I0484654

Making money online

by Start to Monetize

ISBN: 1511652640
ISBN-13: 978-1511652643

Making money online   **4**

Step 1: Build a site   **5**
Idea generation; getting the perfect startup idea   6
Getting a domain name and hosting   10
How to create your website   16
Picking a website template for your CMS   24
Tracking website visitors with statistics   31
Social Media; claiming your urls   34

Step 2: Create content   **41**
Keyword analysis; understanding your future visitors   42
From keywords to content; making the big list   51
How to write articles for your website   54
Adding creative content   60

Step 3: Attract visitors   **65**
Ranking on Google, the hardest work   66
Social Media; from fans to visitors   75

Step 4: Start making money   **80**
Making money with Google Adsense   81
Making money by adding Affiliate Links to your site   88

Step 5: Grow your business   **95**
Becoming an authority in your field   96
Build your network to ensure growth   98

Step 6: Earn more   **100**
How to write an eBook and make money   101
How to create an Online Course and make money   114
Starting an Online Store and making money   123

Conclusion   **133**

Making money online
The 6-step guide to making money with a website

I went through steep learning curves to build and monetize my websites. The information is out there, it always is, but it was scattered and unclear. It was about time a guide was written to explain the steps towards making money online, and here it is.

Making money with a blog or website is hard work, but really, you need to stop hesitating and simply get started. It all starts with an idea (step 1) and from there on it's all about following a set of clear steps towards your end goal; having a successful blog that generates passive income.

The investments you make once you get started with this guide, will start paying off in a matter of weeks. It might take longer for you to be able to quit your daytime job, but that's just a matter of time if you do things right.

Stop hesitating, start now!

Brought to you by: starttomonetize.com

Step 1: Build a site

Welcome to the first step of making money online: Building a Website.

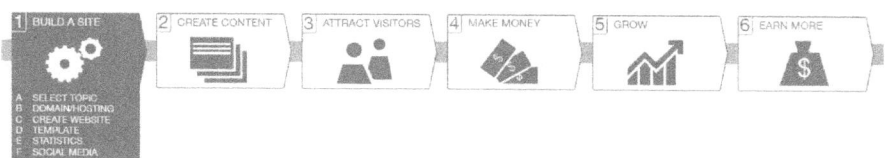

In this first step we start with your startup idea. What is the topic you are passionate about, solves a problem, and most important; leads to profits? Generating ideas and arriving at that one topic is what we start with. Next up is the registration of a domain name and as we will find out, this is an important step for your startup.

Once we have a domain name we can finally start working on creating a website, either by building it with a Content Management System or by using a website builder service. We also need to select a template (the design of your website) and make sure you track your visitors by enabling website statistics. Finally, we register the social media channels for your startup.

Idea generation; getting the perfect startup idea

Welcome to the first and most exciting step of making money online; selecting your startup idea. Since you have looked for- and found this book, chances are you have been walking around with ideas for some time but a) don't know how to proceed, b) hesitate if your idea is the right one, c) don't know which of your ideas is best or d) have no idea yet and need some help to get started. So let's get to it.

Generating ideas

I have come across many people looking to start their online business. Some had the issue of having ten ideas and not knowing which one to pursue (or worse; tried to pursue them all), and some had absolutely no idea at all. Before we seek out ways to generate ideas, let's take a look at different types of startup ideas:

The passionate or knowledgeable
Starting a business because you know more about it than anyone else, or because you are endlessly passionate about the topic.

The problem solver
Starting a business because you see a problem that people experience and you can offer the solution to it.

The profit seeker
Seeing an opportunity that so far, nobody else is pursuing well.

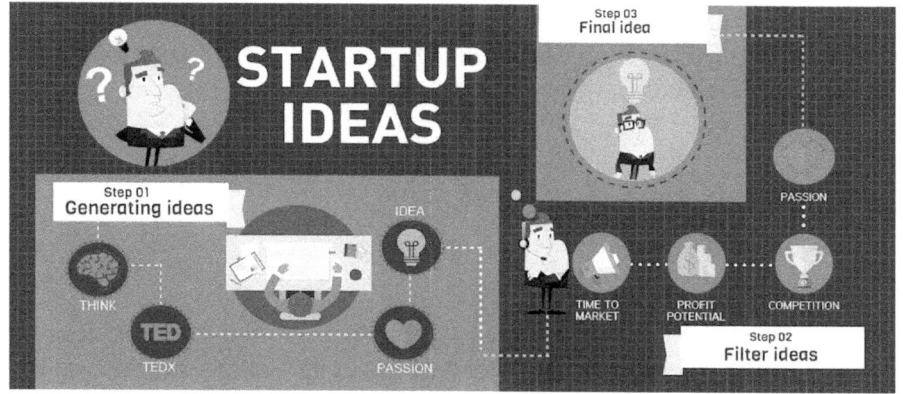

So how do I generate ideas?

I can't generate ideas for you (and most likely you have plenty ideas already), but to give you a few hints:

1. Write down the ideas you have in mind already.
2. Talk to friends, colleagues and anyone you know can inspire you.
3. Attend TEDx talks or similar events near you.
4. Think about the things you are passionate about.
5. Look at what entrepreneurs do who inspire you.
6. Think about problems you experience in every day life.
7. Seek ways to combine your knowledge/passion to solve every day problems.

Every Friday afternoon at work I am struggling, counting down the hours for the weekend to begin. So, I listen to electronic music to help me through. I decided to start a website named BeatsFriday where I help others to beat their last boring hours of the week. I offer them fresh music and a countdown clock to the weekend.
Phil, beatsfriday.com

When I was young, I sailed across the ocean together with my father. One of the best experiences of my life, and I'm doing it again! On my website, I write about my journey to inspire others.
Joris, sailacrosstheocean.com

Selecting your startup idea

Creating the list of ideas was probably not that difficult, right? Forcing yourself to pick one and actually getting started will be much more challenging. Let's have a look at the criteria you should use to select that one final idea:

Time to Market
How much time and effort is required to start with an idea? For your first attempt at making money online it will be wise to select an idea that can be set up in a matter of days, 2 weeks max.

Money making potential
Most would put this point at #1, because this is what it's all about right? Well, I have seen so many people fail to ever launch an idea that to me, it is much more important to select an idea that can be realized relatively quickly. Having said that, the potential of making money is of course important. The potential of money making has much to do with two factors: how many visitors can you attract with this idea, and how much will every visitor be worth? Advertisements for life insurance are worth a lot of money, whereas advertisements for a HDMI cable will be worth much less. The topic you select dictates the potential type of advertisements/affiliates/etc. Thinking ahead, in terms of how you will be able to monetize your startup, is crucial.

Competition
How fierce is the competition for your idea? Are you targeting a niche, or a mass market? In a mass market, you will need to beat much bigger websites that have been around for years. Not only do they have a network they can rely on, they probably have hundreds of incoming links to their homepage, meaning Google will likely

display them far above you in the search results. If you target a niche you have a much bigger chance of establishing yourself and attracting quality visitors. Unless you have a big marketing budget and a lot of experience, you seriously want to target a niche.

Will it last?
Will the idea you have keep you interested and motivated? Will you be able to work on this for hours and days in a row? I promise you, it will be hard work to make money online, so you need to be motivated, and this has a lot to do with what you are spending your time and effort on!

Most people fail in this very first step of selecting an idea, mostly because they hesitate about their idea or lose focus and continue bringing up new ideas. At a certain point, you need to stick with an idea and take the steps needed to realize it. Focus!
Oscar, starttomonetize.com

Idea selected, what's next?

You have put your ideas to the test and finally arrived at one worth pursuing. Congratulations! It is time to think about a name, domain-name and hosting.

Getting a domain name and hosting

Now that we have your startup idea figured out, it's time to get you a name. With the great importance of a good URL, your name will depend on the availability of a domain name instead of the other way around. Let's get started.

I love this step. This is where you turn your idea into reality; once you have claimed your domain name you are officially an entrepreneur and you own your piece of internet property!

What market are you targeting?

Before even discussing domain names, it is important you know which market you are targeting. The majority of people I helped were targeting English speaking visitors worldwide. In this case, there is only one domain name extension that I recommend: a .com. You will find out though that many .com's are already taken. Don't make the mistake of registering a .net or .org instead, you really want a .com if you target worldwide visitors. This has to do with ranking (.com's do better) and with usability (people understand .com domains better than a .net).

In case you target another language things get easier; most Country Code Top-Level Domains (ccTLD) are not nearly as difficult to get. If you are targeting more than one language, invest in registering multiple domain names (a .com for your English site, a .es for Spanish, .de for German, etc.). You don't want your startup to be a success and find out someone took your domain names needed to target other languages/countries. Domains generally cost $10 a year anyway, so think ahead.

Choosing a good domain name is difficult. I can give you a few guidelines or criteria for selecting a domain name, but use your common sense, make a list of available options and ask some of your friends or colleagues for their opinion.

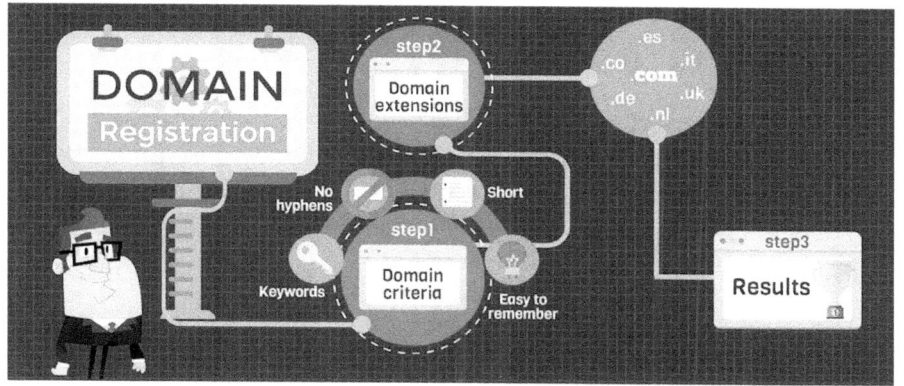

Criteria for choosing a domain name

Selecting a good domain name is crucial for the success of your startup idea. You probably have a name in mind, but is it a good domain name too? Keep these criteria in mind:

Include your important keyword (SEO)
SEO is a term you will come across a lot when building a website, it means Search Engine Optimization (basically, making sure your website gets ranked in Google). Your domain name is still a factor in Google's ranking algorithm, though not as much as it used to be. Why is it still important? Because websites linking to your site will most likely use your domain name as link title (also called anchor text); this is important. So, most often it is a good idea to include the most important keyword for your site in the domain name.

Intuitive
People browsing the internet have virtually no patience. Your domain name is the first thing noted by visitors and so it is important that your domain name resembles what your website offers visitors.

Uniqueness
Make sure your domain name is unique, this will prevent visitors ending up on another website than yours.

Do not use hyphens
Do not use "-" and only use numbers if that really makes sense for your startup idea.

Short is good
You do not want a domain name that nobody can remember or one that you can never print on any business card, right? Keep it powerful by using 15 characters or less.

Easy to spell
Do not use difficult words. Really, you want a simple, easy to remember domain name.

Start searching

Now that you know what you need to keep in mind, start your quest. Checking if a domain name is available can be done using a free whois service. These services check the ownership of a domain you enter, even when the website is offline. One that I particularly like is the one offered by whois.net, as it shows alternatives to options you try. It will help you find a domain name even if most options are unavailable. Don't be put off if you find out most of your desired domains are unavailable; I told you it would be difficult right? Be creative and try many different options. Write down the options that are available and check the criteria above again.

Searching for the domain italianfood.com to see if it is available.

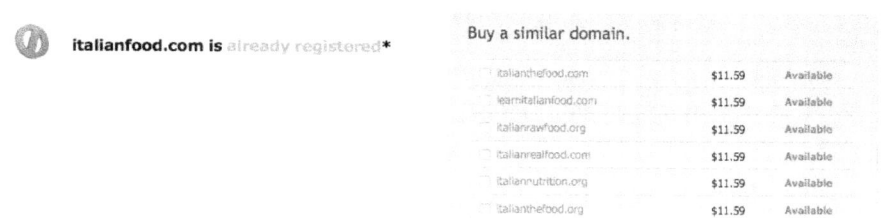

The domain is unavailable, but a few similar domains are available (italianrealfood.com).

Social media URL's

One thing you can try to keep in mind is that eventually, social media will be important to your business. When registering your domain name, it would be convenient to check if these names are also available on your desired social media. I know I am making the domain name quest even more complex by saying this, but it is worth the additional effort.

More information on claiming your social media channels can be found a few pages down.

Found it! Now what?

Found an available domain? Congratulations! Now you need to register it. Most likely, you will need webhosting too (see below) and most often a domain name is included in the price. If you don't need webhosting, a domain name registration company that I always use is InMotion Hosting. Compare the rates with other companies though to see if they offer a good deal.

Choosing your domain name is an absolutely crucial and largely irreversible step. Think it through and involve others to check if you are on the right track!
Oscar, starttomonetize.com

Choosing a webhosting company

Registering a domain name was step one, now you need to decide on a webhosting company. Whether or not you need webhosting depends a little bit on the decisions you take in the next step (building your website), but in 90% of the cases you will need it. If you are unsure, check the next step first and then come back here.

Webhosting, webwhat?
Your domain name is the address, your webhosting is the actual place of your website on the internet. Webhosting is basically a service that rents you a small place on a server, so that visitors that type in your domain name can see the texts and photos you put on your site. Selecting a good webhosting is important, as you want your visitors to be able to visit your website without waiting for pages to load.

Webhosting, what to look for?
Apart from speed, I tend to focus on customer service, because you will need it eventually. After years of experience and many disastrous experiences I put price last in my consideration for

selecting a webhosting company. If you Google for "webhosting company" you will find dozens of companies, look around a bit to compare prices and offers. If you start out with a simple website you are suitable for most shared hosting accounts, only if you have hundreds of visitors a day will you need something more serious. Most hosting companies offer an automated install of WordPress or Joomla! (more about this in the next step, building your website); this might be convenient for you.

For a few years now, I have found my perfect webhosting partner in InMotion Hosting. If you see they have a good deal on hosting, I'd recommend choosing them.

Webhosting companies should be selected on customer service, speed and lastly, price. You don't want to save a few bucks a year and experience your website to be offline while you wait for their staff to finally get around to reading your email.
Oscar, starttomonetize.com

Alright, what's next?

You have selected your domain name and webhosting. Congratulations! It's about time you start making a website.

How to create your website

Welcome to the big step of creating your website. Many options are available, but it all depends on what your requirements are. Start with asking yourself; what do I need for my website? Will it be a simple tutorial website, a page with much visitor interaction, or even a full swing eCommerce website? If you don't have much experience yet, try to keep things simple and don't underestimate the complexity of building a website.

Website; what are your requirements?

Before discussing the options you have in terms of website platforms/systems we need to investigate what it is you need, and what you will need in the foreseeable future. In the previous steps you decided on your startup/website idea and registered a domain name. By now, you have a pretty good idea of what you want. So what is that? What do you need? Some indication:

Basic
Simple but good looking website for adding articles, photos and a contact form.

Intermediate
More complexity; add interaction tools with visitors and other extensions.

Complex
You name it; a website for product comparisons, extended interactions, online shopping, etc.

Trust me when I say that building a website is a potential deal-breaker; the more you want, the more effort it will take. Consider keeping it simple and doing it yourself, or making it complex and outsourcing the work.
Oscar, starttomonetize.com

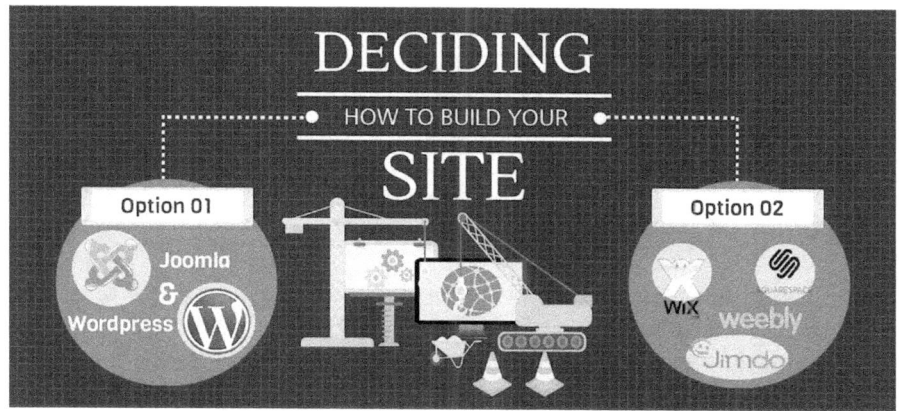

Website options, CMS vs. Website Builder

There are two ways to build a website. The first is to install a Content Management System (CMS) on your webhosting account. The second is to register yourself at a Website Builder Service and assemble the site you want with them.

Building a website with a CMS

A CMS is an open source package that you can download for free. With a CMS you can create an entire website/blog to which many extensions are available, some paid, most are free. Most webhosting companies offer an automated install of CMS systems, so that you don't need to install them yourself and only need to learn how the CMS works.

The big advantage of a CMS is flexibility and endless features; you can really do anything you can think of with a CMS and its available extensions. And they are free! However, it can be daunting to learn your way around the systems and it can be very time consuming. If you have no experience with them so far, you will need to follow some tutorials online to learn how it works.

There are two mainstream, high quality Content Management Systems out there; Joomla! and WordPress. I think they are pretty similar and so it doesn't matter all that much which one you choose.

Joomla!

Joomla! is the system I use for this website, and have been using for all my websites so far. There is a bit of a learning curve in understanding the administration panel, but there are plenty of online tutorials to guide you through the basics. One of Joomla!'s benefits is that it has a big community of developers that create all kinds of extensions to the main system; for Joomla! there are several eCommerce tools (including entire online shop systems), product comparison plugins, newsletter tools, etc. You name it, they have it.

WordPress

WordPress is the most popular CMS for a few years now, mostly because of their focus on blogs. Once you install WordPress, you have a blog you can immediately start working on. But you can do much more with WordPress (more or less the same as with Joomla!). WordPress is a little bit more design-centered and is considered to be simpler than Joomla!, though to me the administration panel is not as intuitive.

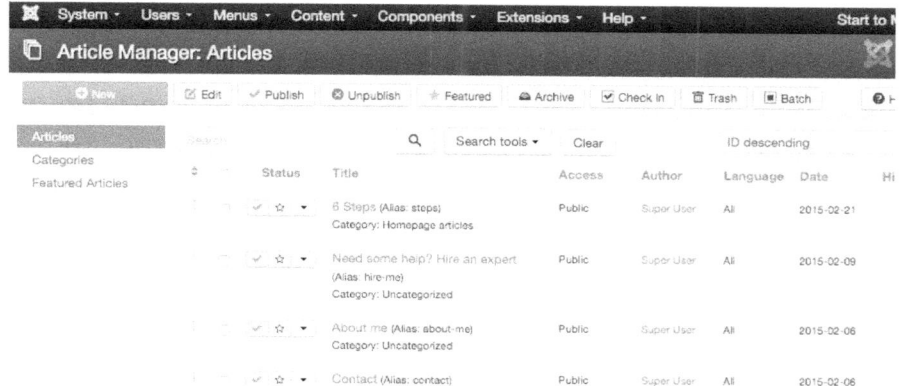

Admin panel of Joomla!

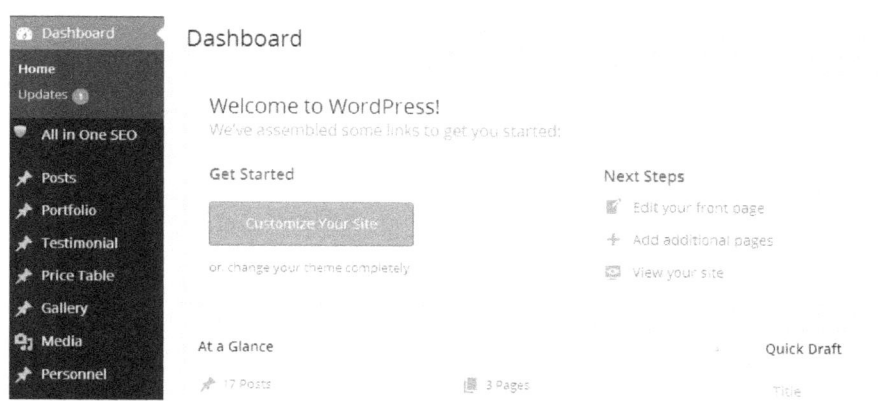

Admin panel of WordPress.

Creating a website with a Website Builder

Website Builders make it much easier for beginners to create a website. But they charge for their services (normally around $100 per year) and you are less flexible in designing and growing your site. Having said that, if you have no experience at building websites, this might be a real intelligent option, enabling you to spend little time on creating a site and lots of time on growing your business.

There are several Website Builders out there, by far the biggest is Wix. SquareSpace is an interesting option as well, with great designs.

Wix

Wix is probably the simplest way out there to create your website. No need to learn any coding and no need to learn a complex administration panel (like with a CMS); you have access to an intuitive drag and drop interface that let's you assemble your site's pages quite easily.

They have many templates available (templates will be discussed on the next page) and since you are paying for their services, you can get support as well. They have a basic eCommerce tool, but if you are into eCommerce (or will be) you really want a CMS and not a Website builder.

SquareSpace

SquareSpace offers beautiful designs and if the design is important for your site, this is your service.
Their editing screen is intuitive and putting together a basic website is straight forward.

Alternatives; Weebly and Jimdo

With Wix and SquareSpace you have enough to choose from, but if you want to check two other services, Weebly and Jimdo are the options.

The Wix edit screen, simple drag and drop interface.

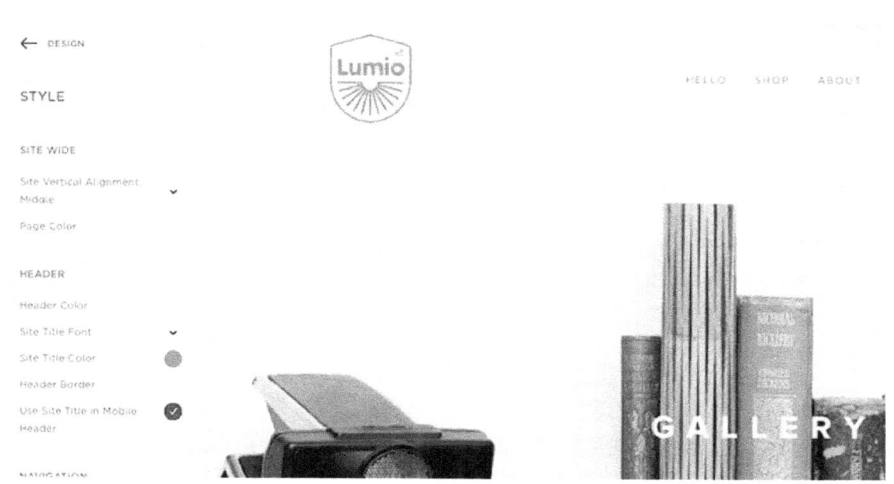

The Squarespace edit screen, also with a simple drag and drop interface.

Making the decision

So how do you choose? It depends mostly on what you want with your site (we talked about that when we discussed the requirements). But, it also depends on your current skills with webdesign and the amount of time you are willing to invest in learning new skills.

To help you make up your mind, I present three scenarios:

You want a simple website and don't have any experience with building websites. And, you want to focus on building your online business, not on building websites. In this case, you shouldn't spend time learning how a CMS works.
Your choice: Website builder

You want a simple website but there is a chance your website will grow and need more work in the foreseeable future. You don't have much experience, but you're willing to invest a few hours acquiring the skills to manage and maintain your website.
Your choice: CMS

You need a complex website and this means you need a CMS. In this case the only question you need to ask yourself is, can you do it yourself or do you need to outsource this part of your business?
Your choice: CMS

The decision ultimately is a tradeoff between focus (should you really put time in learning how to build a website, instead of focusing on growing your online business?) and flexibility (knowing how to build a website will help you a lot, even if you outsource part of the work). If you have the time, I'd say it's worth it to invest in learning to work with a CMS. This will also save you a lot of money on the long term.

Doing it yourself vs. Outsourcing

No matter what method you choose to build your site, the step of building your website will take time and it requires a lot of effort to go through the learning curve. The effort will pay off though, especially considering this is only your first startup idea and probably more will be started eventually.

However, if you have absolutely no skills at designing a website and never made one before, you can consider outsourcing this step entirely. Several platforms exist where you will be able to find someone to make your website. You are still the one that needs to choose which platform you need and most likely if you outsource, it will be Joomla! or WordPress.

So where can you find someone to help you build your website? My favorite place to hire people is Fiverr. For $5 you can order all kinds of basic services and if you need someone to do more, this is also a good place to look around. For a complete website you will probably have to pay at least $100 but possibly much more.

OK, what's next?

You made your decision for either a CMS or a Website Builder.
It is time to think about your website's design; choosing a template.

Picking a website template for your CMS

In the previous step we discussed the options you have for building a website; using a Content Management System (CMS) or a Website Builder service. When you have chosen a Website Builder service you need to select a template that they offer. This page with help you to select a good template for your startup idea, but this page is mostly written for those that work with a CMS like Joomla! or WordPress.

What is a template/theme?

A template (also called a theme) is the design of your website. Your CMS is the system, your template is its look, layout and appearance. Choosing a template is a very important decision for your startup idea, and a really cool one too.

Which template is good for me?

There are literally thousands of templates available for both Joomla! and WordPress. But quality templates are much more rare and it can be incredibly difficult to select the right one, especially if you don't have experience with Content Management Systems.

So what do you need to look for in a template?

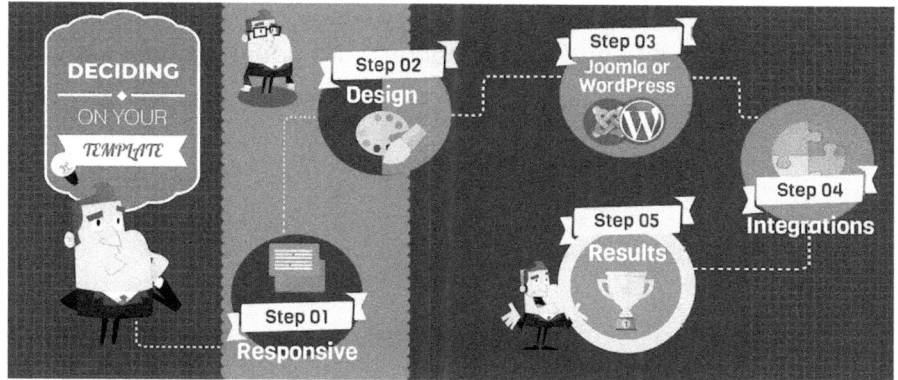

Responsive templates

With the incredible numbers of tablets and smartphones out there, offering a website that adapts its design to the screen size has become a necessity. Over 50% of website traffic is mobile! Your template needs to be flexible and adjustable to all devices; your template needs to be "responsive". Responsive simply means that your template will put modules of your site underneath each other for small screens, instead of next to each other like on big screens. It also means your menu will become a dropdown/miniature version when browsing your site on small screened devices. It is no rocket science, but it is a necessity.

Template design

An obvious criterium, right? Well, also a pretty complex one. Deciding on the design of your website is difficult and you need to be able to put yourself into the heads and minds of your future visitors. What do they look for on your website, and how do you make sure they find it easily? People browsing the internet are incredibly impatient, when landing on your website they decide to stay or not within seconds.

Don't pick a template simply because you think it looks cool; pick a template that is perfect for reaching the goals that you set with your website.

Template versions

Be careful to select a template that was designed for your version of Joomla! or WordPress.

3rd Party integrations

In case you will expand your CMS website with eCommerce extensions, a forum or social media integrations, make sure your template offers these integrations. It will safe you a lot of time not having to do this yourself.

As a designer, my aim was to create an attractive and well designed website. Soon I found out that usability and making sure visitors find what they are looking for is even more important.
Phil, beatsfriday.com

Where to look for quality templates

There are several professionals designing and selling templates and some websites offer templates for free. Only few templates are put together well, so it will help you stick to some of my favorite websites.

Joomla! templates
A few options for Joomla! templates include:

Rockettheme
I love their free template called Afterburner. It is simple, but very fast loading and intuitive. And they have many more templates.

Joomlart
Another good designer of templates, and they have a free template as well called Purity iii. Looks familiar right? Indeed, I used it for this website.

Shape 5
Another option.

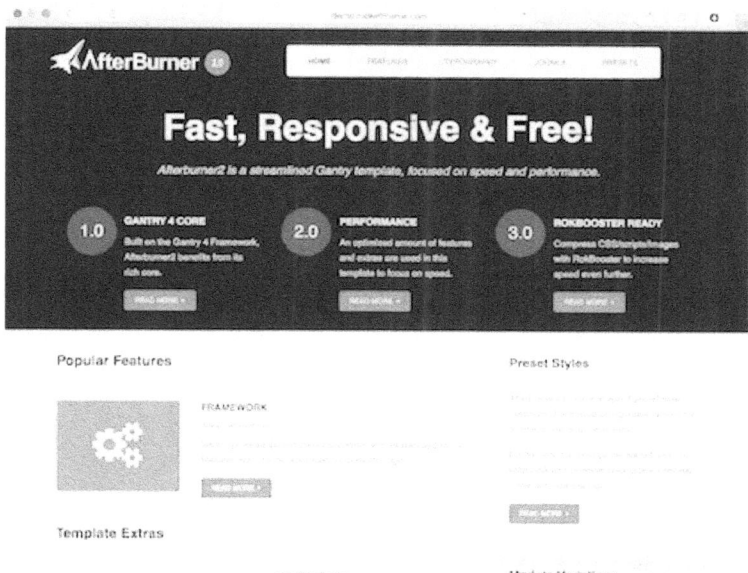

Afterburner template, by RocketTheme

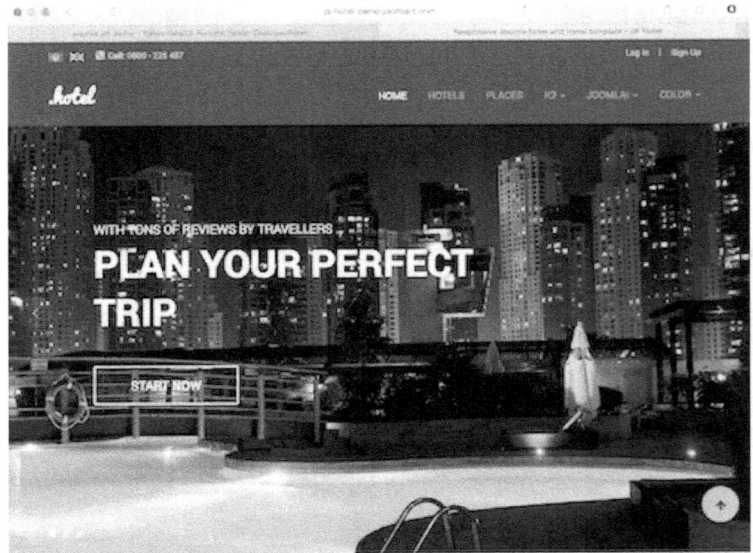

Hotel template, by Joomlart.

WordPress themes (templates)
A few options for WordPress templates include:

WordPress
Many designers added their designs in the WordPress database. It is a bit of a jungle (too many options, too many designers), but fun to look around.

ThemeForest
Large selection of templates.

ElegantThemes
Popular service with a big selection to choose from.

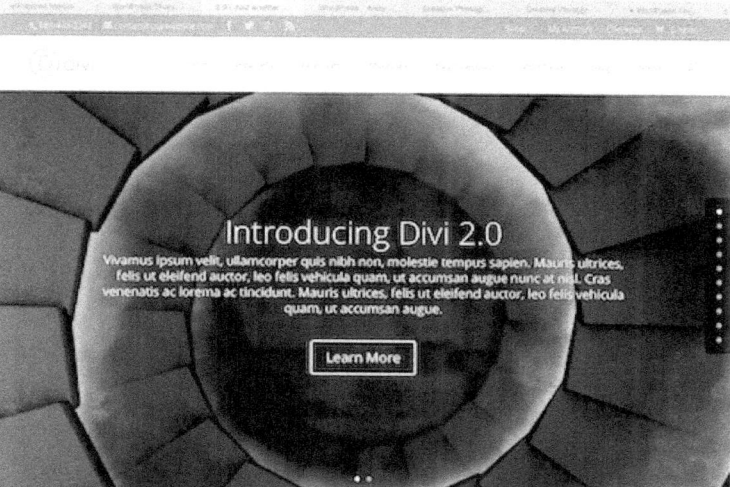

Divi template, by ElegantThemes

The Andy Parker theme, by ThemeForest.

Having a logo designed

The template you select is filled with graphics and content, but you will need to change its logo to suit your website and startup. You can hire a professional designer to design your corporate identity, but this will cost you. I am a big fan of Fiverr, a website where you can have a great logo designed for just $5. Make sure you are clear on what you want for your logo, add some examples you like and let your designer know what the size of your logo should be.

Got my template.

You have decided on the design of your site and selected your template. Well done! Next up; tracking and understanding your visitors with statistics.

Tracking website visitors with statistics

Once your site is up and running you need to start gathering data about your visitors. Who are they, where do they come from, how did they find your website and how do they navigate your site? All this data can be used get to know your customers, so you can improve your site and your online business. But how do we get these insights?

Website statistics

Would I have written this article a decade ago I would have shared dozens of options to gather website statistics. But for a few years now there is one player that dominates the search engine landscape, and one of their most popular services is Google Analytics; the all-in and free website statistics program. There is nothing even close to this program so no need to look any further. Unless you really dislike Google; in that case use Bing and good luck finding an alternative ;-)

So Google Analytics it is, what can I do with it?
You can do more with Analytics than you ever need to. It tracks basic visitor statistics like number of unique visitors, pageviews and time spend on your site, but also how people arrive at your website. A feature I love is that you can easily see how visitors of your site behave; what pages do they spend most time on, what pages do they open after arriving at the homepage, etc. These insights are highly valuable to you as webmaster, enabling you to keep improving the content on your site to deliver your visitors what they are looking for.

How do I install Google Analytics?
You need to register for an account at Google and register for Analytics. When registering they will show you a piece of code that needs to be added to your site; this is the tracking code. Most CMS

templates and Website Builders let you paste this code in a designated setting, making it very easy to enable Google Analytics on your account.

Google Analytics interface

Google Webmaster

Another service Google offers is named Webmaster. This is a free service that shows you all kinds of data useful to optimize your site: how your site is ranking in Google, any problems that the Google bots find on your site and an overview of other websites linking to your site.

While you are registering for Analytics, make sure to also register for Webmaster.

Google Webmaster tools.

Alright, what's next?

You have quality statistics on your visitors from now on. Congratulations! Let's start claiming your Social Media.

Social Media; claiming your urls

Social Media channels like Facebook, Twitter, YouTube, Instagram and Google+ can be of great importance to your online startup. It helps to build your brand, to attract awareness, in getting visitors and sometimes to make money directly. It will depend a little bit on your specific startup idea to decide which channels matter, but be sure to take this step serious. Social Media matters.

Which Social Media exist?

There are literally hundreds. So let's proceed to the next question.

Which Social Media are important to me?

A much better question, because in most cases only a few Social Media matter to you. It depends greatly on what your startup idea is, who your potential visitors/customers are and what your goals are. Let's investigate the Social Media networks one by one so you can decide which ones matter to you.

Facebook

The biggest and most important of them all. This is an important place to build your brand and a potentially great source of traffic.

Claiming your page at Facebook is easy and just takes a few minutes. Getting Facebook fans is the difficult part and you will need to be creative and willing to put a lot of effort in it to grow. If your startup idea can be graphically presented (think nature, photography, cars or simply beautiful things) you will be able to attract a lot of fans simply by posting photos regularly. It will be much more difficult to get fans if this is not the case. Things that work on Facebook are the things people like to share and like.

Turning Facebook fans into website visitors or even into customers can be tricky, because Facebook tries to keep most traffic inside its network. But, if you fan base is large enough, it can be substantial anyway. My experience is that a photo with a thousand likes, provide about 2000-3000 visits to my site.

Facebook offers methods to grow your fan base by paying for it. This can work, but be critical if the investment will be worth it. If you decide to invest in getting fans, make sure you are targeting people that are your potential customers. Getting fans from India is much cheaper than getting fans from the US, but can you monetize fans from India?

Google+

Small, much smaller than Facebook, but important to some niches. Besides, Google uses its social network as a ranking factor for their normal search results. If you're big on Google+ that helps your site attract organic traffic from Google's search results as well.

Growing your Google+ page is quite similar to the strategies I suggest for Facebook; Google+ is probably even more centered around graphics/images/movies. Turning your fans into website visitors is relatively straight forward, assuming your website has enough interesting content.

The Facebook channel of Nike.

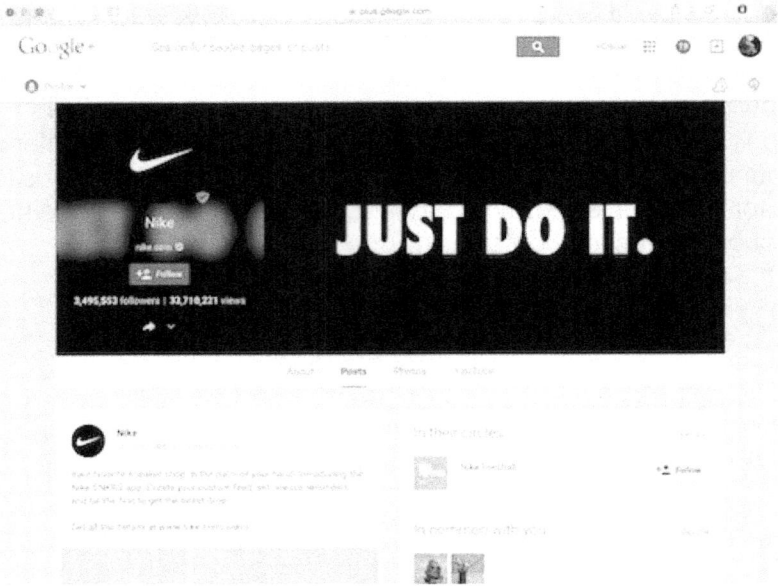

Google+ channel of Nike

Twitter

The social network centered around short messages, Twitter is big and important. No matter what your startup idea is, you better be on it because your future customers will use this channel to communicate with (and about) you.
Growing your followers base has a lot to do with being interesting to follow. You will need to share interesting stuff (links to cool articles, posting on events you are visiting, etc) to grow and keep your following up to date. Turning followers into your website visitors is easy and so this Social Network pays off.

LinkedIn

The business/corporate network. Depending on your startup idea, this can be super important, or not important at all.I find it hard to get a substantial following on LinkedIn, so if it is important to your idea, be prepared to put quite some effort in this.

Instagram
Very important if your startup idea has anything to do with design or lifestyle. Instagram is super graphically oriented and a great platform to build your brand on. However, it's almost impossible to turn fans into website visitors; so Instagram is only interesting if you are building a brand or a personal network.

Pinterest
A bit similar to Instagram and mostly of interest when you are into design, lifestyle, decoration or nature. While your efforts on this network will result in limited traffic at best, the network as a whole can be very important for gaining visitors to your site. The good thing is that you don't need to do much for that, because your website visitors can pin your images to their boards and generate traffic for you.

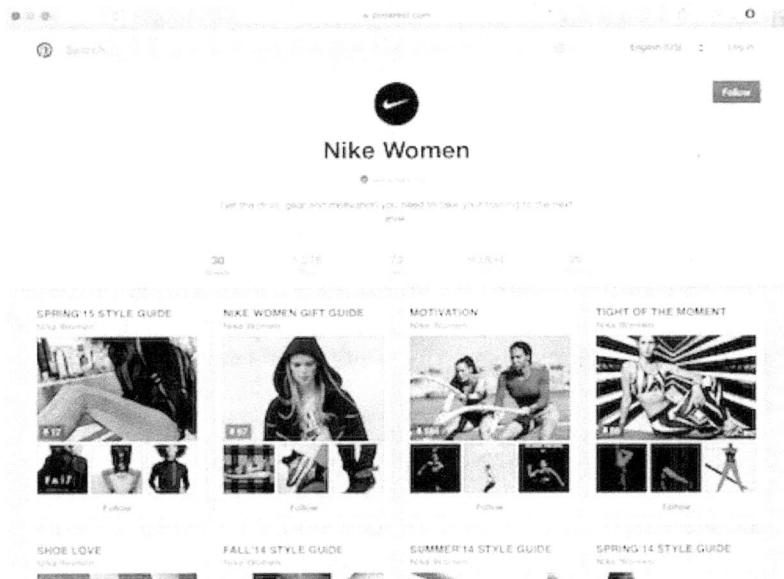

The Pinterest channel of Nike.

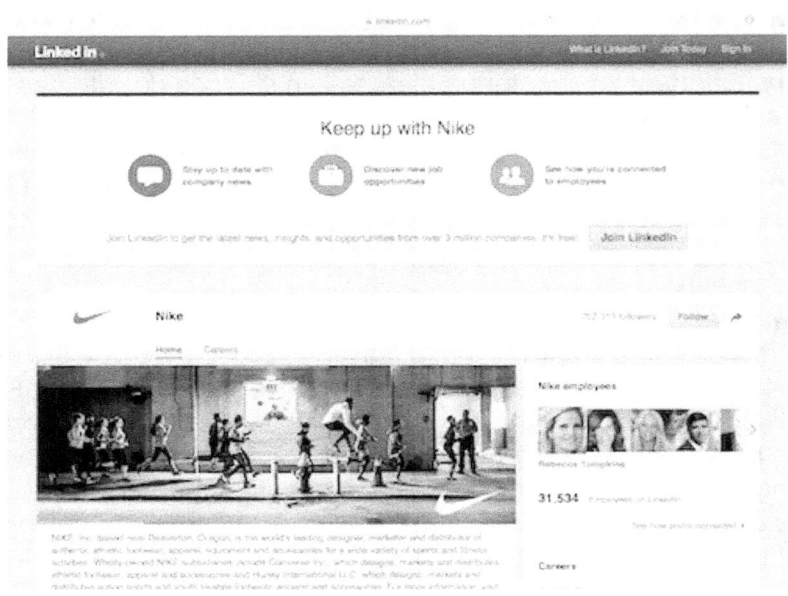

The Linkedin channel of Nike

YouTube

Is it a Social Network? Perhaps not, but for most startup ideas this channel will eventually be important to you. YouTube can be used to grow your brand and to make some money with advertisements, though you will need a lot of views to make a living out of it. Generating traffic from your movies to your site is difficult, as of course YouTube tries to keep the visitors inside their platform. To register your YouTube channel you first need a Google+ account.

I have invested much time in Social Media and my Facebook page has over 100k fans. This has proven to be one of the best investments of my time, as every new article I write, the eBook I published and movies I create are instantly popular and well visited. And my personal network has grown significantly. Social Media turned out to be crucial to my website's success.
Oscar, bonsaiempire.com

How do I claim my Social Media urls / pages?

In most cases (Facebook, Google+, YouTube, LinkedIn) you don't need to register new accounts for your startups. Assuming you have a personal account at these Social Media channels already, you can easily start your startup fanpage/channel. You will need to register your Social Media accounts separately for Twitter, Pinterest and Instagram.

When claiming these channels, you probably want to use the same urls as your main domain name. The same principles apply here; keep it simple, intuitive and easy to remember. Read more about these criteria at the choosing my domain name chapter.

Since the registration processes change quite often at the social networks, I suggest you use Google to find out how claiming your urls work for the specific Social Media channels.

Setting up my appearance on Social Media

Once you register your startup at the different Social Media channels, you will be taken through a few steps to set up your appearance there. Use your logo (or a personal image, depending on what your startup idea is) for the profile image and set up your details including your website url. Google+ will require you to proof your website is linked to the page you just registered on Google+, if you registered your site on Google Webmaster this is done automatically.

We discuss in more detail how to benefit from your Social Media efforts in step 3 (attracting visitors: how to turn fans into visitors on Social Media).

Social Media, check!

You have your Social Media all set up.
Congratulations! Time to proceed to Step 2.

Step 2: Create content

Welcome to step two of making money online: Creating Content.

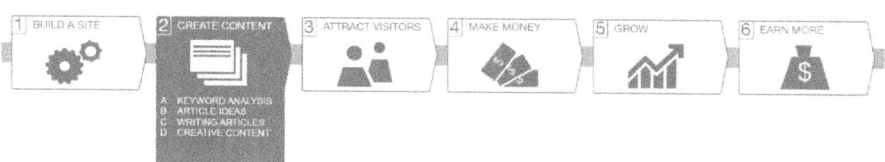

In this step we start with an analysis of your website's topic to reveal its most important keywords; this keyword analysis will be useful to come up with a list of article ideas, topics that you will need to generate content about.

The next step is to start writing articles that are suitable for online-reading and that have good structure. Apart from writing I encourage you to add creative content as well, like infographics, charts or even movies.

Keyword analysis; understanding your future visitors

Welcome to the Geek step. This is where I will guide you through a straightforward process of analyzing your startup idea to find out what topics are central to your idea, a step absolutely crucial to the success of your entire website. It will enable you to create content people are looking for and it will help you get that content ranked well in Google.

Keyword analysis, what?

In the previous step you have done your share of brainstorming and soul-searching to arrive at your startup idea. You probably know a lot about this topic already, but I am sure there are many related topics that you don't have in mind. All these related topics I will from here on call "keywords".

You probably can't tell what your top 10 keywords are, right? And you have no idea how much search traffic these terms potentially have, right? Time to do the ~~math~~ analysis.

Finding out what your keywords are

Open an excel/numbers sheet and take some time to think about your startup idea, than answer these questions:

What is the central topic of your startup?
Add it to the top row of your excel.

What are the important sub-topics?
Add them vertically to your excel.

What are the most important sub-sub-topics?
Add them vertically to your excel.

What are important related topics?
Also add these.

A simplified example

My topic is: Italian food recipes

My important sub-topics are Spaghetti, Lasagna, Pizza, Risotto, Gnocchi and Tiramisu

Some of the sub-sub topics for Pizza would be: Pizza dough, Pizza sauce, Pizza toppings, Thin crust Pizza, etc.

A few related topics: Spanish food recipes, Greek food recipes, Mediterranean food recipes, but also: Italian food restaurant, Italian food ingredients, Italian food history, etc.

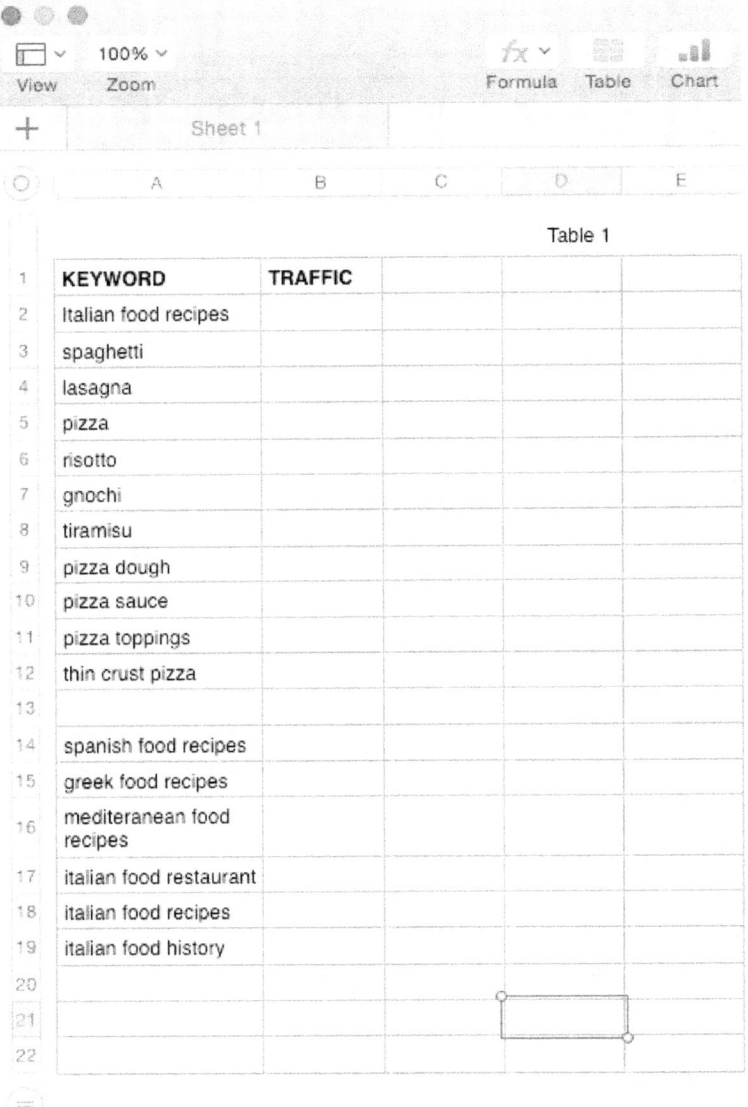

KEYWORD	TRAFFIC			
Italian food recipes				
spaghetti				
lasagna				
pizza				
risotto				
gnochi				
tiramisu				
pizza dough				
pizza sauce				
pizza toppings				
thin crust pizza				
spanish food recipes				
greek food recipes				
mediteranean food recipes				
italian food restaurant				
italian food recipes				
italian food history				

The excel/numbers sheet in use

This XML file does not appear to have any style information associat

```
- <toplevel>
  - <CompleteSuggestion>
      <suggestion data="pizza hut"/>
    </CompleteSuggestion>
  - <CompleteSuggestion>
      <suggestion data="pizza hut coupons"/>
    </CompleteSuggestion>
  - <CompleteSuggestion>
      <suggestion data="pizza dough recipe"/>
    </CompleteSuggestion>
  - <CompleteSuggestion>
      <suggestion data="pizza hut near me"/>
    </CompleteSuggestion>
  - <CompleteSuggestion>
      <suggestion data="pizza hut coupon code"/>
    </CompleteSuggestion>
  - <CompleteSuggestion>
      <suggestion data="pizza ranch"/>
    </CompleteSuggestion>
  - <CompleteSuggestion>
      <suggestion data="pizza luce"/>
    </CompleteSuggestion>
  - <CompleteSuggestion>
      <suggestion data="pizza near me"/>
    </CompleteSuggestion>
  - <CompleteSuggestion>
      <suggestion data="pizza sauce recipe"/>
    </CompleteSuggestion>
  - <CompleteSuggestion>
      <suggestion data="pizza guys"/>
    </CompleteSuggestion>
```

Search suggestions by Google

Adding more keywords

I am sure you have done your mini assignment and came up with a lot of sub-topics and sub-sub-topics. Now it's time to get analytical and check the data. It is time to start adding more keywords by asking Google for help. You probably know that when you type a search phrase in Google, it starts giving you suggestions.

Try entering "Italian food recipes"; immediately you see Google giving you suggestions like "italian food recipes with chicken" and "italian food recipes pasta". This is useful data, I forgot about the chicken! Now try "Pizza"; depending on where you live, you probably see a lot of "Pizza Hut" and local Pizza restaurant names. That's not helping.

Time to scale things up a bit. There is a little known trick in which you can get these suggestions from Google in neat lists. Try this URL:

http://suggestqueries.google.com/complete/search?
output=toolbar&hl=en&q=pizza

Now you get a list of the 10 most relevant suggestions to the term "Pizza". Note that Firefox shows the list well, but Safari sometimes shows a blank screen. Try another browser if this link doesn't work.

If Pizza is a very important keyword to my website, and I will be adding a lot of content about Pizza, I need more keywords on this sub-topic. Actually, I want to know about what people can possibly search for that is related to pizza. There is a clever way to get many more keywords, by adding the letters of the alphabet one by one in front of, but also at the back of the search term. So use terms like "a Pizza", "b Pizza" as well as "Pizza c", "Pizza d", etc.

Sounds strange, it doesn't make sense, so just try it and you'll see what I mean. Use these urls to do that:

http://suggestqueries.google.com/complete/search?
output=toolbar&hl=en&q=pizzad

http://suggestqueries.google.com/complete/search?
output=toolbar&hl=en&q=apizza&cp=1

Actually, this is a lot of work. And I only investigated the word "Pizza" and still have to get the same data for "Pasta", "Spaghetti", "Lasagna", and many more. But this is absolutely vital information for me, because I need to get into the minds of my potential/future website visitors. I need to get the data so I know for sure I am not missing important topics.

There is a really convenient website that automates some of the steps, called UberSuggest. Unfortunately they do this only for finding terms behind the keyword (not in front of it), so you will have to do part of the work manually still. Go to the website of UberSuggest.com to see how it works.

Collect all the keywords from all your topics, if possible try some of the related topics you came up with earlier as well. I am looking for an excel document with hundreds, of not thousands of keywords.

Analyzing your keywords

Alright, you have your list of keywords ready and you are sure you are not missing important topics. Now it is time to ask Google how much traffic these keywords can generate (the search volume). You will need to get a Google Adwords account to check this, but that is not much work. Step by step:

1. Register at Google Adwords.
2. After registering, login and on the Adwords homepage click on "Tools" and then on "Keyword planner".
3. Then click on "Get search volume for a list of keywords...".
4. Open your excel and copy all your keywords into the blank field at Adwords.
5. Adept the targeting to your potential website visitors. If that is "English speakers" do not put English as language but instead, target the countries that you focus on (like the USA, UK, etc). This will help you get better data out of it.
6. Click on "Get search volume".
7. You now see a list of your keywords and their search volumes.
8. Download the data and open it, sort by descending. If you can not download it in a neat excel (only as CSV) have it added to your Google Drive and then export as XLS.

Nice! Now we have data we can use.

You have an accurate overview of what keywords/topics are important to your website, so that you know what you need to write about. You still need to apply common sense though, as some keywords attract a lot of traffic but are not central to your startup idea. We will do that in the next step.

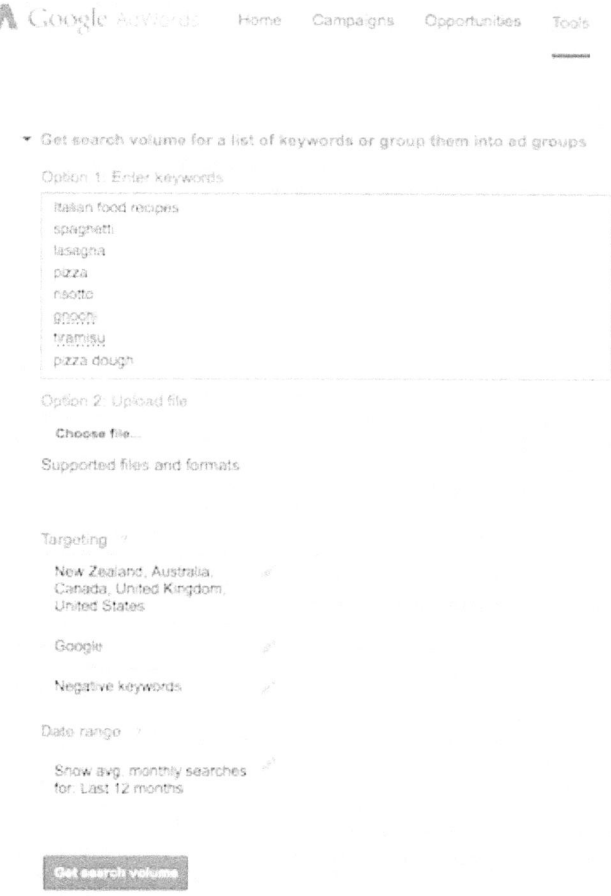

Search volume check

Enter keywords

Italian food recipes, spaghetti, lasagna, pizza, risotto, gnochi, tiramisu,

Ad group ideas   Keyword ideas

Keyword (by relevance)	Avg. monthly searches ?
pizza	1,000,000
lasagna	165,000
tiramisu	165,000
risotto	135,000
spaghetti	110,000
pizza dough	60,500
pizza toppings	22,200
pizza sauce	14,800
Italian food recipes	6,600

Results using Google AdWords

Keywords analyzed.

You have your list of keywords and the next step is to decide what topics you will write about.

From keywords to content; making the big list

In the previous step (keyword analysis) we arrived at a big list of keywords and their search volumes. Some startup websites don't need to create content in the form of articles, but without doubt, most do. So let's take the keyword analysis one step further to create our to-do list in terms of content that we need to create.

From keywords to content

Open your keywords excel sheet and sort search volume by descending. This is the big list of keywords that matter to your startup idea. But right now, it is just an endless list of words and we need to decipher it to get to a list of unifying topics.

Using our previous example

My topic was: Italian food recipes
My important sub-topics were Spaghetti, Lasagna, Pizza, Risotto, Gnocchi and Tiramisu

I take my excel sheet with the keyword data I generated and start working from the top to start structuring the keywords into my (previously established) sub-topics. Most likely, several keywords can not be categorized into my sub-topics. This means I am either missing categories, or these keywords simply don't make sense for my website.

Using my Italian food recipes as example; I have a lot of keywords with traffic on Meatballs. Did I really forget about meatballs? This new sub-topic is added to my list pronto! And the same applies to many other categories, including Bruschetta, Cannelloni, Wine, etc.

I will also discard keywords if I feel they don't match well. Either way, my sub-topics list is growing.

Not only would I be adding sub-topics by analyzing my keywords, I will also be adding sub-sub-topics. What if I see a lot of traffic on keywords like "salami pizza" and "pizza funghi", these are all sensible sub-sub-topics for the Pizza sub-topic right? Keep adding to that topics list.

The topics list

Finally, after analyzing my keywords and structuring it into sub-topics, I arrive at a topics list that from now on I will simply call my future website's structure.

With my Italian food recipes example I will have hundreds, if not thousands of potential topics on my list. This is just an example though and in this example I would surely have to focus on a niche (or spend the rest of my life writing).

Let's hope you have been more clever and you selected a niche; apart from your main topic you might have about four sub-topics and each of those sub-topics have a few sub-sub-topics. You have a website structure now and you're ready to start creating content.

Honestly, I had no idea what content I needed to create for my startup website. Having analyzed the keywords central to my idea, and structuring them into topics, really helped.
Nils, trustmeimafysiotherapist.com

Apart from using data to get to a to-do list of creating content, also select topics you are simply passionate about. Always write about stuff you love or are knowledgeable about. If it doesn't match with your main content, add a blog to your site where you can add it. Use that passion!
Oscar, starttomonetize.com

I have a list, now what?

You have your website structure in mind, and a list of topics, let's start writing articles then!

How to write articles for your website

Most money making guru's would have named this article "SEO writing" or "Making your articles SEO proof". SEO means Search Engine Optimization and put simple, it means optimizing your site to rank well in Google. So why am I naming this article "How to write articles for your website"? Because your articles are not written for Google, your articles are written for visitors. They need to like your work, be able to scan your texts quickly as well as read your entire texts conveniently.

Writing for a website

As I have mentioned earlier, people browsing the internet are lazy and impatient. After arriving at this chapter, you have probably scanned the titles and read part of the introduction, before deciding to continue reading. Why? Because it is easy to hit the 'back' button (on a website) and open another page if you feel this page is not exactly what you were looking for. So how do you write for the internet?

Adding the right title

Research shows that the title is the single most important factor for visitors in deciding to go to your site. This decision is made both before they land on your site (as the title is shown on search results in Google) as well as after landing on your site (is this indeed what I am looking for, or should I go back to Google and check another page?). A good title interests your potential visitors and should cover the content of your article well.

Scanning vs reading

Your articles should be written to suit two very different types of readers: those who actually read your entire text and those who quickly scan your article and read only one paragraph with information they were specifically looking for. Even those who read your entire article most likely first scan through it to see if this is indeed what they are looking for. So, your article needs to be scan-proof. How? By adding clear structure in your article.

h1. Heading Secondary text

h2. Heading Secondary text

h3. Heading Secondary text

h4. Heading Secondary text

h5. Heading Secondary text

Media Object

Media heading

64x64

Cras sit amet nibh libero, in gravida nulla. Nulla vel metu at, tempus viverra turpis. Fusce condimentum nunc ac r

Media heading

64x64

Cras sit amet nibh libero, in gravida nulla. Nulla vel metu at, tempus viverra turpis. Fusce condimentum nunc ac r

Adding structure to articles using headings and objects.

The importance of structure

Structuring your articles is important as it helps your visitors to scan your text, decide quickly if you offer what they are looking for, let's them read easily through your text and to help them remember your main points. Articles can be structured by adding clear hierarchy in terms of titles and subtitles, adding graphics, adding bullet and numbered points, adding quotes and varying typography. But structure also means that you discuss a topic in a logical order, with an introduction, your main points and a concluding text. Before you write an article, think about the structure first!

Tone and style

Choosing the right tone and style of writing for the internet most often means that you need to be personal and upbeat. Only very few websites use a strictly formal tone, think about large corporate websites and other 'serious content'. Keep your audience in mind and adept accordingly.

Make it graphical

A picture is worth a thousand words, and a movie is worth a thousand pictures. Such a cliche, I know, but its true! It depends a little bit on your topic, but you can be sure that adding graphics, images, flowcharts, drawings, infographics and movies will greatly improve your article. Especially those scanning your article will focus on the graphics you have added.

I explain a lot of techniques on my website, so over the years I have been adding more and more photos, graphics and movies. I found out this dramatically increased traffic to my pages as well as the average time spend on those pages. Graphics matter!
Oscar, bonsaiempire.com

Writing SEO (Search Engine Optimized texts)

In the introduction I made it clear you should write keeping your readers in mind, not Google. Absolutely true, but... Would it hurt to at least keep Google in mind a little bit? Not at all. So what does writing a SEO text mean?

In the previous two articles ("keyword analysis, understanding your visitors" and from "keywords to content") I used the example of Italian Food recipes as topic of my site. Let's apply this example once again.

I analyzed my keywords and found out that one of my most important sub-topics was "Pizza".

Looking at my keywords list I found terms with a lot of search volume like "Salami pizza", "The best salami sausage for Pizza" and "What ingredients go well with Salami on Pizza".

I was already planning to write an article on "Salami Pizza", but I just found out that people are apparently interested in which Salami sausage should be used and what ingredients can be used on a Salami Pizza. In my article on "Salami Pizza" perhaps I can add a paragraph on what Salami sausages are recommended, as well as adding a paragraph on ingredients that go well with salami.

I do this for two reasons; I know people are interested in these topics, but I also know there is a lot of search volume for this, so I better write about it right? Not only will I write about it, I will make sure to include the keyword "The best salami sausage for Pizza" in my subtitle. For my visitor (who is interested in this paragraph and needs to find it while scanning my text) and for Google (so that Google knows I offer information about this).

Check the subtitles of the chapter you are reading right now; noticed I added "Writing SEO" in this text as a subtitle? Exactly!

Example of a well structured article

Ah, you made it this far? Then think about it; did you read this chapter entirely? Or just parts? Or did you only scan it?

Instead of giving you an example of a structured article, try it yourself. Browse through this book and check the structure of 5 pages. Scan through them and spend 10 seconds per page. Which article do you like most? Why?

Probably you have selected an article that is not too long, has graphics, has many titles and subtitles and probably some bullet points as well as a quote. The richer the content, the better.

What I usually do when writing new articles is to create a structure first (I add my title and subtitles, add an empty quote box and add empty bullet points) and than start writing. This way I force myself to create well structured articles that can be easily scanned.
Oscar, starttomonetize.com

I know how to write now.

Well done, and good luck with the actual writing.
When you're done, proceed with adding creative content.

Adding creative content

We all agree that a picture is worth a thousand words. Why is it then, that people create mostly text-based articles? Sure, some topics can be presented graphically easier than others, but it still doesn't make sense. Clearly, you can get ahead of your competition by adding creative content, like infographics, flow diagrams and movies.

Adding creative content to your site

Creative content can be a great feature for your site and set you apart from your competitors. What I hear a lot is that people find it difficult to come up with ideas how they can make their website more graphical, but it really isn't that difficult. Even topics that you would expect to be text-oriented can benefit substantially from graphics.

Let's look at a few examples to help you:

Italian Food recipes
This one is easy right? I can think of stunning food photos, graphics of what ingredients you need to make pasta sauce, movies or an infographic that tells me about the basics of the Italian cuisine.

Web scripting languages (HTML, PHP, etc.)
A more challenging example. But still, I can think of many examples of how to present it creatively. Perhaps an infographic to explain me the very basics of HTML and its history, or a flow diagram to show the most important features of PHP.

How to do your bookkeeping
Nice! This one is tricky. I might hire a graphic designer to create illustrations of the steps involved at bookkeeping (keeping receipts, a filled binder, my software and a calculator) so that I can make my text a bit less 'boring' by adding graphics. Or I would create a

graphic with a calendar with the yearly tasks on it. Or again, an infographic about the steps involved in bookkeeping.

If this didn't help, go to Google images and type in the topic you would like to add creative content for. Most likely, you will get some ideas there. And you can even overcome your creativity block by outsourcing it; ask a graphic designer to create graphics for your article and let him decide how to do it.

Types of creative content

Alright, let's look at the different types of creative and graphical content:

Infographics
My favorite way of presenting information. Infographics are tall graphics that explain data in an almost purely graphical way; the key is to use as little text as possible. It helps your visitors understand the basics of a topic, before diving into it.

BONSAI *Styles*

Bonsai are traditionally styled to reflect many situations.

These styles range from the calm and stately F style characterized by a straight vertical trunk to which is inspired by trees clinging for their lives f mountain.

Other designs reflect a tree's endurance to ove persistent elements such as in Literati and Wind

FORMAL UPRIGHT   INFORMAL UPRIGHT   SLANTING   WINDSWEPT

Part of an infographic

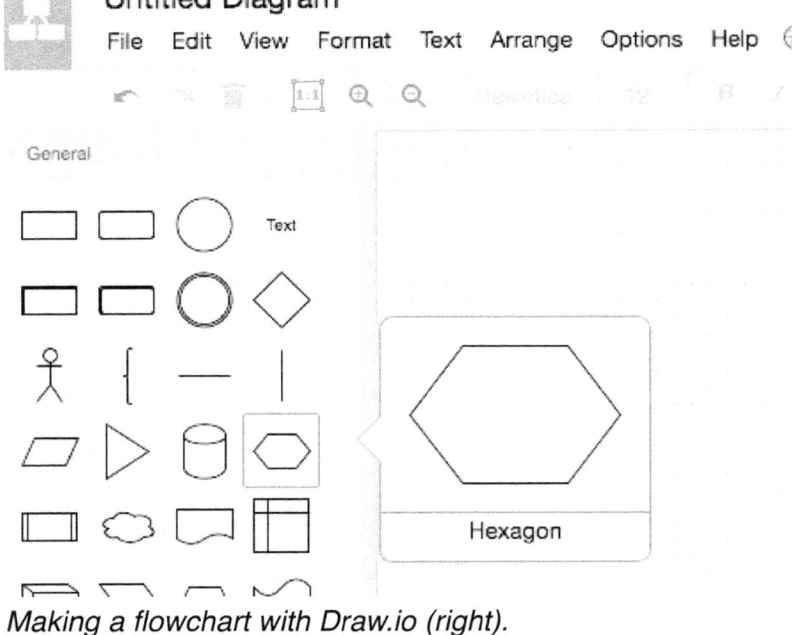

Making a flowchart with Draw.io (right).

Stunning visuals
Visuals are graphics that complement your texts. Look at the homepage of my Start to Monetize website; there are a lot of visuals there to help make the text more obvious. Think about the topics you write about, and how you can enrich those texts with graphics and icons. WeGraphics is a website with some cool examples, but it might make more sense to hire a graphic designer on Fiverr.

Flow charts
A great way to structure your articles (or even entire website) is to add flow diagrams. You find them on my site, showing you in what step you currently are. There are several platforms that enable you to create flow charts for free, one of them is Draw.io.

Movies
Possibly the best, surely the most difficult graphic to create. Movies help to explain complex content and make your website more personal and trustworthy. Movies can take shape as a tutorial (with you explaining things) but also as introductions (just look at my homepage movie).

I hired a graphic designer to make an infographic for me. Immediately after adding it to my site it got featured on Reddit and many blogs covered it, all adding links to my site. This turned out to be the best link strategy ever and even better, my website visitors loved it!
Oscar, bonsaiempire.com

Where can I hire someone to create my graphics?

My favorite platform is Fiverr, and you can literally find anything here. Most gigs cost $5, more complex jobs will cost more. Just browse their website and I'm sure you will be inspired. The movie on this website's homepage was also made by people from Fiverr (the voiceover and the movie were separate gigs).

Got graphics, what's next?

I hope I inspired you to add creative content!
You have now completed step 2! Next up; attracting visitors.

Step 3: Attract visitors

Welcome to the third step of making money online: Attracting Visitors.

Attracting visitors to your website has a lot to do with how well it ranks on Google's search results. This is why we start with information as well as a how-to guide on Ranking your site on Google.

Of course there are many other ways to get visitors on your site, an important one will be your Social Media channels.

Ranking on Google, the hardest work

There are many ways to attract traffic to your site, but for most startups the potential traffic from search engines (read: Google) is most significant. Getting traffic from Google means you need to rank high on search results that are relevant to your content. But how does that work?

Ranking high on Google, what does that mean?

Google uses a highly complex and ever changing algorithm that decides which results rank high, and which ones not. Simply creating quality content on your site will not ensure you attract traffic from Google. Let's take a look at what most experts think are important factors of Google's algorithm, factors that you need to start taking very serious!

Factors influencing rankings on Google

Incoming links
By far the most important factor is the number of incoming links to your site, and to its subpages. Google sees these links as signs of trust; if other websites link to you, you must be doing something right. Simple as that? Well, the science behind using links as ranking factor is incredibly complex and Google is doing very well at understanding which links mean more than others. I will discuss this point in detail below.

Anchor text
The anchor text has something to do with the links pointing to your site. If I have a page on how to make Pizza, most links from other websites to my site (these are called external links) will probably say something like "click here to learn how to make pizza" or "pizza recipe". These two examples are the anchor texts, and Google uses these to understand and check the content of my website. The anchor texts are important pieces of information to Google.

Social media
This factor has been gaining importance for some time now and we can all understand why. If a website is shared and liked on social media, that must mean that it is interesting. Google gives its own social network (Google+) most weight, but Facebook likes and shares are also very important. We focus on this in the next step; using your social media to gain traffic.

Keyword usage
This is the first ranking factor that you can manage directly. If you understand what people are looking for (by analyzing your keywords), you can write your content with SEO (search engine optimization) in mind. Say, you write about "Salami pizza", in this case it is important to use important keywords (like "salami pizza", "best salami sausages for pizza" or "ingredients that match well with salami") in your article's titles and text. It has a lot to do with what we learned in the previous chapter (writing articles for the internet).

Loading time

An important factor to keep in mind is your site's loading time. The higher your loading time, the worse your ranking. Google penalizes slow websites. So make sure your website is fast enough by choosing a good template (it is nice to have hundreds of pictures, but think about what that does to your loading times) and by choosing a good webhosting company.

Conclusion; how to rank well?

Put very simple, if you want to rank your website's content high on Google you need to create quality content that is optimized for SEO, and you need to get others to link to your work. We discussed creating SEO optimized content in the previous article (writing articles for the internet), so let's learn more about how to get quality links to your website.

Ranking your site is simple, but hard work. Optimize your website's content, grow your social media and exchange quality links.
Oscar, starttomonetize.com

Link building to start ranking well

You need incoming links to your content, from external websites. Preferably with good anchor texts. How?

First we need to have a look at what links are valuable and which ones aren't. I am walking you through the basics, if you want more, I highly recommend Moz' SEO guide. Let's get started, the following is mostly common sense, but here goes.

Linkbuilding, what kind of links do you need?

Authority / Quality
If an authoritative/famous website links to your site, that means a lot more than when a little known (or even spammy) website links to you. Links from spam websites can even result in a penalty, so you need to be picky in choosing your link partners. The authority of a website can be established by looking up its Google Page Rank or by looking at the Page Authority using the Moz Open Site Explorer.

Relatedness
Very similar to the authority of a website is the concept of relatedness. If a website links to you that is unrelated to your topic, this link is much less valuable than when a highly related website links to you.

Quantity
The quantity of external links to your site is obviously of great importance. Assuming you manage to prevent spam-links, we can safely say that more is better.

Anchor text
We talked about this above. The text that external website use in their link to you is of great importance to Google.

Locality

It depends a bit on the type of website, but in many cases, it matters where your links come from. Websites have IP addresses so Google always knows where they are hosted/located. Having many links from just a few IP addresses is worth less than having links from different IP addresses. If you run a local store, local links (from that state or country) will matter more.

Social links

We talked about this as well; social media likes and shares matter increasingly.

Strategies for linkbuilding

We have two main strategies for building links, and anyone taking this step serious will have to follow both:

Strategy 1. Creating great content

By now, you understand why you need good content to beat the competition. The internet is crowded with millions of websites and to win, you need to be better, smarter and more dedicated. When your content is great, people will link to it without any effort from your side.

So what content is share-worthy? What content has the potential to go viral? The most linked pieces of content I have come across are great quality tutorials, infographics and other graphical works of wonder. People like graphics, they really do. Content going viral often has to do with something being genuinely interesting to many people, newsworthy or simply something funny.

To persuade visitors to link to your content you need to make it easy for them. Give them a code-snippet so they can add your infographic directly to their site, with a link to the original (your website). Explain how your YouTube movie can be easily embedded on other websites and add social sharing buttons to your content.

Strategy 2. Outreach

You thought creating quality content was hard work? Reaching out to other websites to suggest link exchanges is potentially much more work. But as always, efforts pay off, especially on the long run. If you do your outreach campaign (contacting webmasters to ask for a links exchange) smart, you maximize your return on effort.

Before you start reaching out to potential linkpartners, you need to decide which content you want to promote. I try to promote my homepage as well as a few of the important subpages, but this 'mix' depends on your situation. If you are in a specialized niche, ranking your homepage on your most important keyword is possible. But if you target a mass market with a lot of competition, it makes sense to try to rank a few of your subpages on very specific keywords first. You won't be able to compete on a general keyword in a mass market, but you can compete on specific keywords or keyphrases.

Who should I target as link partner?

Most likely, you know what websites are important in your industry or niche. But you will need more, many more in fact, because only 10-20% of the people you request to exchange links with will actually do this. Open an excel/numbers sheet on your computer and create three columns: url, email, name. Now let's get started:

Competitors
Which websites are important in your industry / niche? Write the url, email and preferably the name of a contact person in your excel, using one row per website.

Investigate their links
There are smart ways to analyze the websites of your competitors and find out who link to them. I always use Open Site Explorer for this (with a free account). Surf to their website and fill in the url of your first competitor. You now see a list of their incoming links, ranked by importance. This data is super! Surf to the first, say, 20 websites linking to your competitors and again, gather all the data to your excel sheet. Repeat this step for all your competitors.

Google for more
Probably you have a pretty big list by now, but we want more. Another way to find potential link partners is to simply use Google and search for the most important keywords you want to rank on. Open the first, say, 20 websites per keyword and collect their data to your excel.

How should I ask them?

Now that you have created an excel sheet with the url, email and names of a lot of potential link partners we can start your linkbuilding campaign. But you need to be creative to maximize the return on effort; the email you send to potential link partners needs to be well thought through. Perhaps before you 'pop the question' try to be in touch with the most important potential linkpartners through social media, at events, etc. If people know you, or even like you, exchanging links is much easier.

So what should I keep in mind when sending link request emails?

Make it personal
The style of your email should, in most cases, be personal and, in all cases, honest. For the most important potential link partners, adept your emails by adding a question about something you read on their site, about something he/she said on a presentation, etc. Or turn it around, first ask these questions, create a conversation, and then 'pop the question'. Always make it personal!

Email subject
The email subject is something you need to think about carefully. What subject will interest the reader, a general subject like "Exchanging links" or something else?

Address your email
You collected the names of your potential link partners, which was a lot of extra work, but sending an email to an actual person works much better.

What's in it for them
Yes, you are asking for a favor when you propose to exchange links, but try to keep in mind "what's in it for them". You will of course add a reciprocal link, but can you do anything else that s valuable to them?

Keeping track of your ranking

Now that you know how ranking on Google works, and started your linkbuilding efforts, it is time to track your rankings.

I track the ranking of my 25 most important keywords on Google with a very convenient and free tool named SERP checker. Register on their site and add your website and its most important keywords. Also select the Google version that is important to you (Google.com for example, or Google.co.uk). With these settings you can conveniently track your rankings once per month. If some of your rankings do well, while others drop, you know what to focus on.

Alright, what's next?

You now know how to rank on Google and you understand that linkbuilding is hard work but crucial to the success of your site. Next: Social media.

Social Media; from fans to visitors

You have your Social Media channels registered, but now you need to start working them to get something out of it. You want to build your brand, engage with your fans, get important insights and convert them into your website's visitors, ultimately making money. Most Social Media try to keep their visitors inside their network though, so it won't be easy.

Setting goals for your Social Media channels

At this point, you will have to decide what goals you want to achieve with your Social Media efforts. Your options:

Building your brand
By being active on Social Media you make sure your name, logo and ideas get recognized.

Building your network
Social Media, especially LinkedIn but also Facebook are great places to build your personal network.

Engaging with fans for insights

By actively engaging with your following you can gain a lot of insights, which can be used to improve your website or your startup concept.

Getting visitors

By sharing your website and its content you can attract visitors to your site. If you're big on Social Media, this can be a substantial amount of traffic.

Work on your Google ranking

For most websites, this is a side effect of pursuing one of the other goals, but it can be a goal in it selves. Being big on Social Media can help your site rank well in Google.

How do I grow my Social Media channels?

Being big on Social Media is hard work. In the chapter about claiming your social media channels you can find more information about growing on the most important Social Media networks.

You can also choose to pay to increase your amount of fans/followers. This can work, but be critical in deciding whether or not the investment is worth it. If you decide to invest in getting fans, make sure you are targeting people that are your potential customers. Getting fans from India is much cheaper than getting fans from the US, but can you monetize them?

Another method to grow on Social Media is to run giveaways and competitions. Be careful to respect the guidelines that Social Media give when you are organizing a giveaway though, the rules can be quite strict. And you need to realize that most fans you gain from a giveaway are gone afterwards, or are at least harder to monetize than fans that follow you because they like your work.

I have invested much time in Social Media and my Facebook page has over 100k fans. This has proven to be one of the best investments of my time, as every new article I write, the eBook I published some time ago and movies I create are instantly popular and well visited. And my personal network has grown significantly. Social Media turned out to be crucial to my website's success.
Oscar, bonsaiempire.com

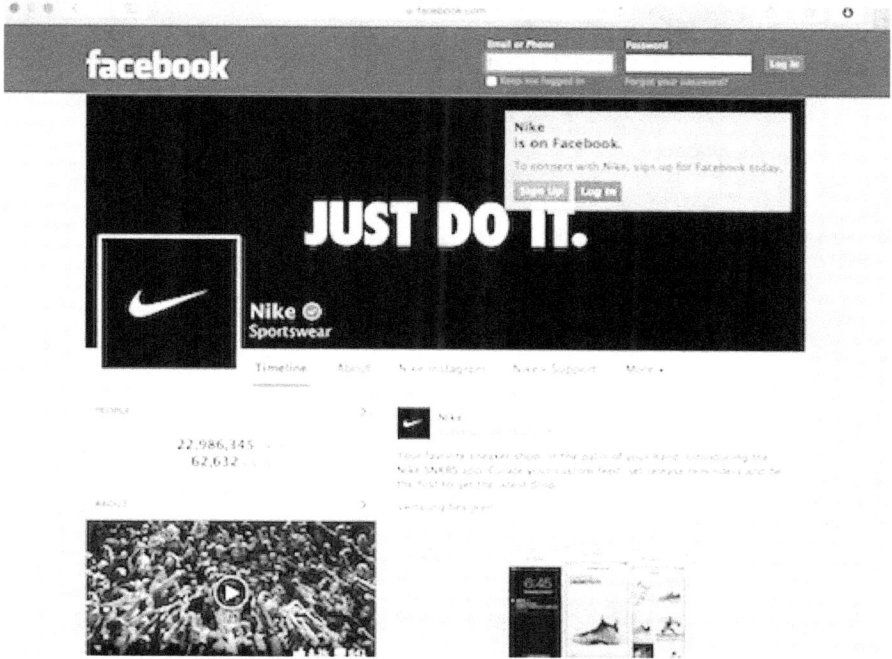

The Facebook channel of Nike.

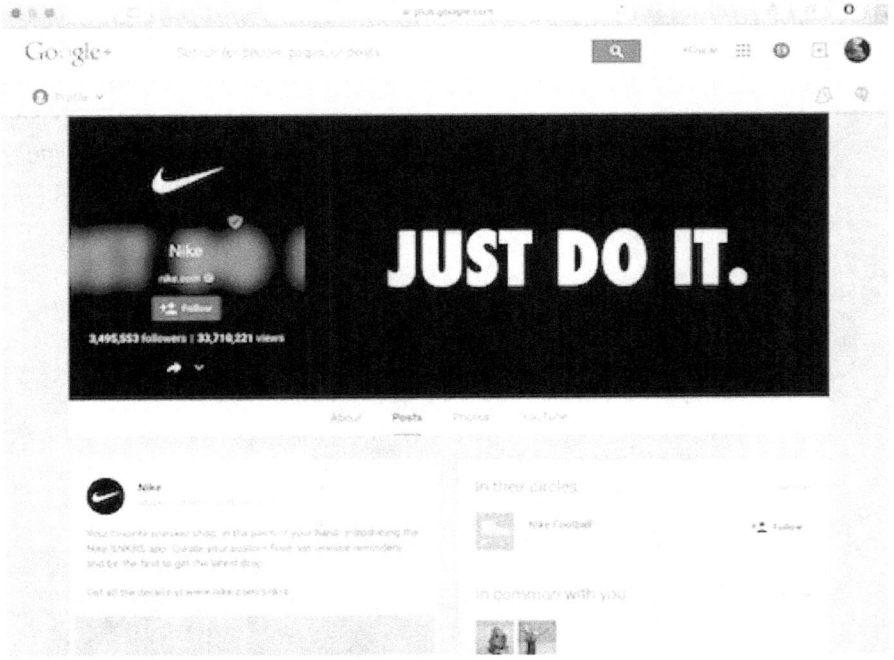

The Google+ channel of Nike

How do I turn fans into visitors?

The answer to this question depends on what Social Network you are referring to.

In most cases (Facebook, Google+ and Twitter) you can post photos and text messages with working links to one of your pages. This works pretty well in fact, but the more you do this, the less clicks you will generate. Key is to balance the type of posts you share. I'd say one in four posts should contain a working link. With Facebook you can turn fans into customers, by starting an online shop within the Facebook website. Check Shopify or StoreFront.

Other networks are more closed, especially Instagram. With Instagram no links can be added to posts, so the only way you generate traffic is by persuading fans to type in your domain name and surf to your website. Since Instagram is mostly mobile based, that is not happening.

If it is traffic you seek, focus on Facebook. If you are building your brand name or your personal network, the other networks are all recommended.

Social Media; check!

You now know how to build and utilize your Social Media channels. Next step; starting to make money with your website.

Step 4: Start making money

Welcome to step four: the basics of Making Money with your site

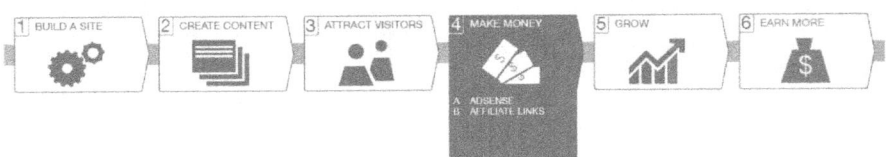

Finally you reach the step where we start monetizing your website. The starting point is Google AdSense. With AdSense you allow Google to place advertisements on your website, often the most profitable way to monetize it.

Another way to make money with your site is to add affiliate links inside your articles.

Making money with Google Adsense

At this point you have a website, filled with content and your visitor stats are on the rise. It is about time you start making money with your website! The obvious start is to add Google AdSense to your website. But make sure to read the entire article before getting started, Google is strict about who they let into their program and you have only one shot!

What is Google AdSense?

Before we answer that question we need to look at how Google brings together supply and demand for advertisements. We start with a very short intro to Google AdWords.

Google AdWords

Google makes a lot of money with showing advertisements on their search results. Often, the first three results are ads (sponsored results) and Google gets paid per click. Advertisers can set up their campaign using the network that Google created, named AdWords. In their campaigns, advertisers let Google know what keywords they target and how much they are willing to pay per click. Google AdWords is a continuous auction system, the more advertisers are willing to pay for certain keywords, the higher the clicks are worth. And the highest bids get top place and attract most traffic.

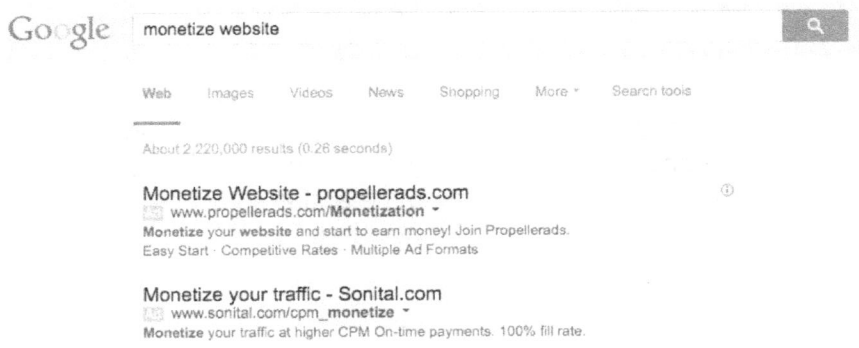

Ads that appear when searching on Google.com

Google AdSense

Apart from advertisements on their own search engine results, Google offers advertisers a substantial network of websites (called publishers) where they can also advertise. This network is contributed by webmasters like you and me. This supply side of the advertisement market is called AdSense. So how does making money with AdSense work for me as a webmaster?

Basically, I reserve a small part of my website for Google and let them decide which advertisements they display there. For every click on these ads, I get paid my share (this share is 68%, Google takes 32%). The more clicks and the higher the value per click, the more money I make. It is that simple.

The beauty of AdSense lies in the fact that Google's network of both supply (their search results and their network of associated websites) and demand (the advertisers) is huge. The bigger the network, the better Google can target the advertisements and the more people click on ads. The other brilliance of AdSense has to do with how they decide which ads to display. They analyze the pages on your site but also the browsing history of your visitors, this makes that the ads shown on your site are highly targeted and therefore, effective.

An ad I place on one of my websites

How much can I earn with AdSense ads?

This depends on two things. The number of clicks and the value per click.

The number of clicks is related to the amount of visitors your site has and to how you place your ads. Placing your ads where all your visitors will see them will help improve the Click-Through Ratio (CTR), but this can also scare your visitors away (too many, or too annoying ads are irritating). I am personally very conservative with this and put my visitors first and my ads last, literally.

The value per click depends on which ads are shown and this has much to do with your visitors and your niche. Your clicks will be worth a lot if you have a website about life insurance (maybe even a dollar or more per click). Why? Because the advertisers (life insurance sellers) are willing to pay a lot as their product has a long-term and high profit margin. If you have a website about Italian food recipes, your clicks will be worth much less (for most industries, expect to get paid 5 to 15 cents per click). Google calls the value per click "cost per click (CPC)".

Say you have a website with 10.000 pageviews per day. Your CTR is 1% (that's pretty good) because your ads are well placed, but not too annoying for your visitors. You will generate 100 clicks per day. With an average CPC of 15 cents your website is making $15 per day.
Oscar, starttomonetize.com

How do I join the Google AdSense program?

Google is picky who they let into their program and they set strict rules. Applying can only be done once, so be careful to respect the rules because you don't want to mess this up. The rules:

1. Before you apply, your website must consist of at least 10-20 pages.
2. You are not allowed to click or ask people to click on your ads
3. Your site has no pornographic content and it does not violate copyright laws.
4. You may only have one AdSense account.

Ready? Apply for AdSense now and then continue reading.

How do I add AdSense to my site?

Once accepted by Google, you have access to your AdSense account. Login and go to "My Ads" and click on "New ad unit". You can now create your ad and select the ad size you prefer. Google will hand you a piece of code that needs to be inserted into your site, either by adding it manually or by using a plugin (these are available for Joomla!, Wordpress and all Site Builders).

Recommended ad sizes, the leaderboard is the best performing ad.

How can I increase my AdSense earnings?

Simply adding AdSense to your site is not enough. You will need to think carefully about where to show the ads on your site and also which ad-sizes you select. More important even is to start testing what works for your site. Experiment with your ad sizes and with where you place the ads.

Rule of thumb

Ad size: the leaderboard (728x90) is one of the most effective ad sizes.

Ad placement: either on the left, above the fold (the fold is the part of the page visitors see without scrolling down), or all the way down at the footer of your site (once people reach the bottom of your site, it takes effort to scroll back up so this is a good place for ads).

Google will help you to optimize your revenue by giving you advice on a Scorecard. Their advice is not always useful, but be sure to try and test their recommendations.

Scorecard

Last updated: February 10

Revenue optimization

●●●

Multi-screen

●●●●●

Site health

●●●●

The scorecard is an optimization tool for publishers. We do not take any account actions based on your scores.

Google AdSense scorecard helps to increase your earnings

Word of warning

AdSense income tends to fluctuate significantly, some months are better than others. I have experienced a big drop in income twice, for no apparent reason. Also, sometimes people are banned from AdSense because of "potentially fraudulent click activity". If you steer away from anything even remotely linked to fraudulent activity you will probably be fine, but what I am saying is, don't rely solely on Google AdSense to monetize your website. Think about ways to complement your AdSense income, for example by adding affiliate links to your site, writing an eBook or starting a webshop.

Alternatives to Google AdSense

There are several alternative programs to AdSense, but unless you have a lot of traffic, most of these alternatives will unfortunately generate much less income. This does depend on the niche you are in though, so I definitely recommend trying these alternatives as soon as you make good money with AdSense.

Chitika
Chitika is mentioned by most experts as the only real alternative to AdSense. If your site has a lot of traffic you can get into their Gold program, which will result in better performance. My personal experience is that earnings are significantly lower than those with AdSense, but as I said before this depends a lot on the niche you are in. Try it and know it.

InfoLinks
One alternative I come across a lot is InfoLinks. They offer ads but also in-text ads (which means some of the words inside your articles reveal ads).

BuySellAds
Another alternative, aimed at high traffic websites.

Google AdSense is brilliant, everyone with visitors can make money with their website. This is a stimulant for webmasters to keep creating great content and contribute to the internet.
Oscar, starttomonetize.com

AdSense placed, what's next?

You now make money with your website, awesome!
Next up; adding affiliate links to your site to increase your income.

Making money by adding Affiliate Links to your site

Your website is growing in popularity and your visitor stats are doing well. Most likely you started monetizing your website by adding Google AdSense, but now you seek ways to complement your income. Adding Affiliate Links can be a great way to do so.

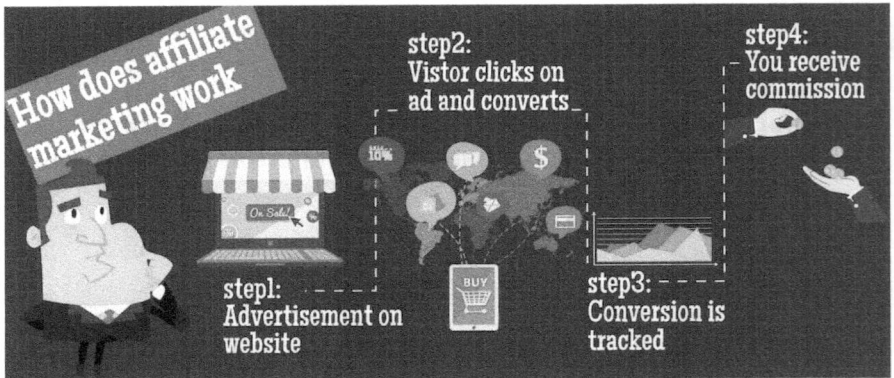

What is Affiliate Marketing?

Affiliate Marketing revolves around commissions. As a website owner, you can promote and even sell products for another business, and get paid for the revenue you generate. You can select what business and which products you promote. The beauty is in its simplicity (you don't need to invest in creating and selling products, you only need to promote products) and in the resulting win-win situation (you make money, your partner make money and your visitor finds his product).

Sounds easy, right? Well, yes and no. It is incredibly easy to set up, but earning a substantial amount of money with it is difficult. You will need to experiment and find out what works for you.

The biggest advice I can give you is to be very careful at what products you promote, and how you do this. I only promote products/companies that I am familiar with and I never push my visitors to buy something. Not following this advice can greatly damage your reputation.
Oscar, starttomonetize.com

Payment terms

There are different methods of Affiliate Marketing available to you:

Pay per Sale
This is the most common method and if someone refers to Affiliate Marketing, this is what they most likely point at. You get your commission when one of your visitors clicked on an affiliate link on your site and purchases products from your partner. Only when the purchase is completed will you get your share. Depending on what agreement you have with your partner, you get your share for the product you promoted on your site, or for the entire order that is made.

Pay per Lead
In some industries it makes sense to reward webmasters for generating leads instead of sales. A lead can be many things, but most often this means that after clicking one of your affiliate links, your visitor leaves his contact details with your partner. You get a fixed revenue per lead.

Pay per Click
Very similar to Google AdSense is the Pay per Click option; you get paid per click.

Selecting your Affiliate partner / Affiliate Marketing programs

There are tons of programs where you can register and select Affiliate companies and products. I am sharing with you the most important ones:

Amazon
Amazon is absolutely huge and offers pretty much anything you can think of. Because your visitors will know and trust Amazon, promoting them is relatively easy. Amazon's commission program is named Associates. They offer a commission depending on how many revenue you generate, normally this means anything between 5 - 10%. This is less than you will get elsewhere.

CJ Affiliate
CJ is short for Commission Junction and they offer the biggest network of Affiliates. Their reporting tools are very convenient and will help you in your experiments to find out what works best for your site. If you don't find what you want to promote on your site here, good luck finding it elsewhere :-)

Share a Sale
Similar to CJ Affiliate, this is a big network with all the possible partners and products you will need. Their reporting is not as good though, so if you are just getting started perhaps you better try CJ first.

LinkShare (Rakuten)
LinkShare has been around forever but is not as big as CJ and Share a Sale. A feature I like about their service is Ad Rotation. This means you can let LinkShare decide which ads work best for your site. If you don't mind spending time experimenting, pick one of the others.

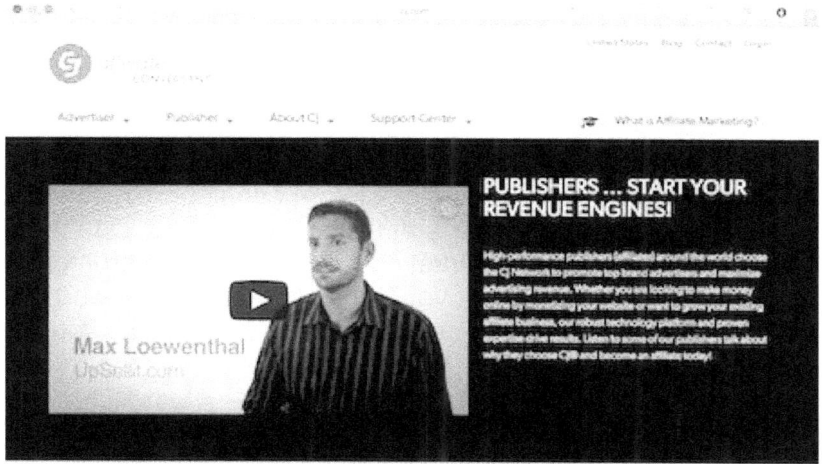

Affiliate program CJ.

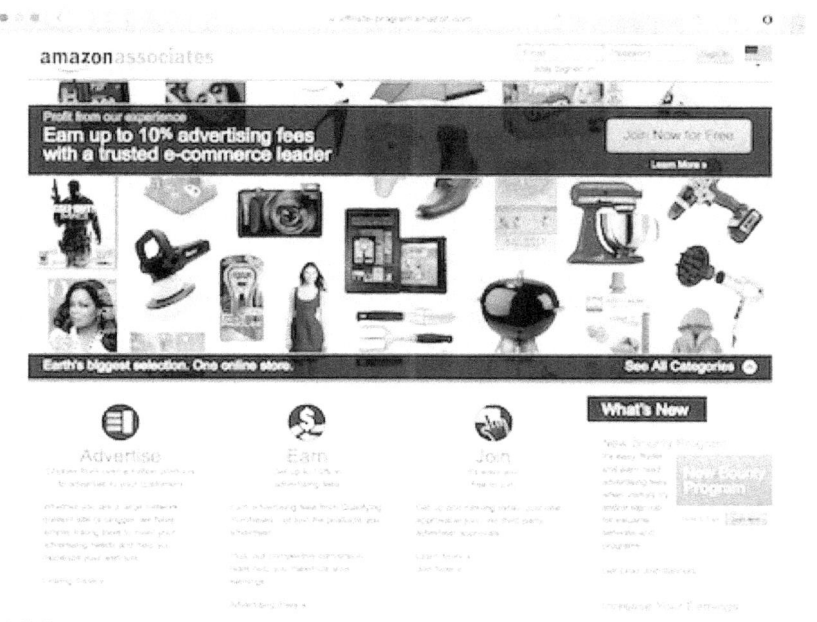

Affiliate program Amazon

How to make money with Affiliate Links

As I mentioned in the introduction, information about making money with Affiliate Marketing is quite difficult to generalize. One thing is obvious though; Affiliate Marketing works best if you promote products that you use and love. The more you are involved with these products, the better you will be at explaining why your visitors need them too.

You will need to experiment with what products do well on your site and how you place your Affiliate Links. Most important, you need to balance your quest for monetization with keeping your visitors happy.

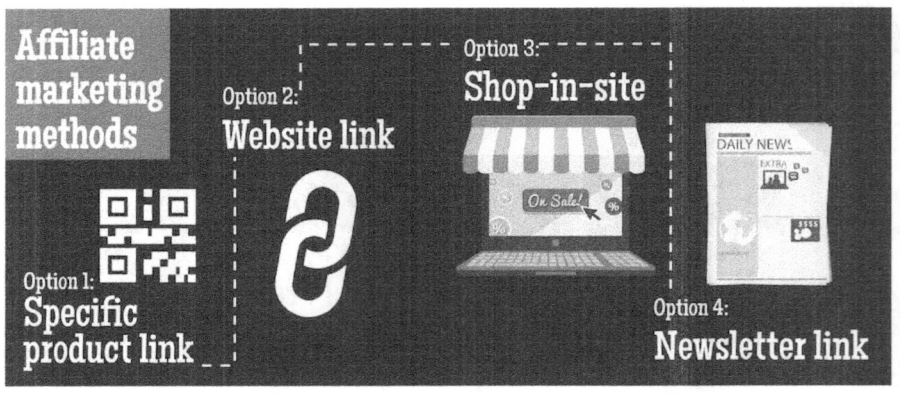

Affiliate Marketing methods

There are several options available to add Affiliate Links to your site:

Specific product link

You have a product you like and in one of your articles you talk about it. This is the perfect example of how Affiliate Marketing can do wonders; you recommend a product and add a link to a store that sells it. The link is of course an Affiliate Link, so if one of your visitors clicks it and ends up purchasing the product, you get a commission. It depends on your partner agreement if you also get a share on other products that your visitor might purchase.

Website link

Instead of linking to an exact product, you link to a website that sells products/services. If your visitor buys anything through your referral, you get your share.

Shop-in-site

Depending on what your startup is doing exactly, this could be a very good option. Instead of recommending a product/service on an external website, you show products inside your own website, using a Shop-in-site. Amazon offers this option and it is quite easy to set up.

Newsletter

Specific product links and website links can also be added to your newsletters, and if your newsletters are popular, this could be very lucrative. Do check your agreement if you are allowed to do so though.

What products to offer

Affiliate Marketing has grown so big that it is safe to say that anything that sells on the internet can be promoted/sold from your website with Affiliate Links. The key to success is to offer the right products at the right spots. Take a good look at your website and decide, per page, what would fit there. I personally only add Affiliate Links if it really makes sense and only promote services/products that I like. This prevents visitors being annoyed because my website is too commercial. Finally, I can't recommend Pat Flynn's website enough for more information on all this, especially for his great posts on Affiliate Marketing.

On my website I talk about some of the products I love and if possible I use Affiliate Links to monetize these products. These are the best performing Affiliate Links on my site.
Nils, trustmeimapsychotherapist.com

Affiliate Marketing; got it!

Well done! You are making great progress in monetizing your website. Next up, bringing your startup to the next level. Time to grow big!

Step 5: Grow your business

Welcome to the fifth step of making money online: Growing your Business.

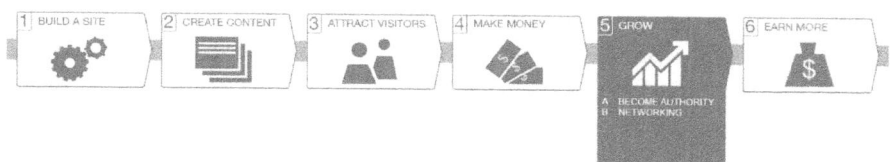

By now you have created your website and started its monetization. But to grow further you and your website need to become an authority in your niche. Only with a certain level of authority will you be able to exchange links and set up partnerships.

Building your network is another way to enable further growth of your website.

Becoming an authority in your field

Now that you have your website all set up and started to make money online, it is time to start thinking ahead. At this point, growing your business further is not about getting more links and not about creating more content, it is about becoming an authority in your field. Once you reach a certain level of authority, it will be much easier to exchange links, set up partnerships and keep building your dream.

How to gain authority in your niche

Becoming an authority has much to do with your personal as well as your startup's branding. You will need to find ways to have people blog about you, write about your startup and trust your expert opinion. It will depend largely on what niche you are in, but think about it, what do you need to do to build your brand? Here's a few options to get you started:

Guest blogging
Guest blogging is one of the first things you need to think about at this point. Yes, you will be creating content for others (maybe even for your competitors), but it can do much good. You reach new audiences, share what you have to say and probably you are allowed to mention your latest cool piece of content on your website.

But how do you become a guest blogger? You will need to use your personal network and pitch your proposition as a win-win situation. Send them an article you think they might like, or an outline, to generate interest in your work.

If your personal network is not yet established, read my chapter on how to build your network. In this case, try to get in touch through Social Media and start creating a relationship. Ask questions through email or discuss a point that is of interest to both you and the blog owner; until you are comfortable with making your pitch.

Writing an eBook

Writing an eBook can be a great way to build your brand, but it all depends on the quality of your content. If it's good and you manage to promote your eBook well, you might just reach audiences you'd never be able to reach with your website. Read my chapter on making money with selling an eBook for more information.

My website was doing fine but at a certain point it became hard to keep it growing. I started putting more effort in growing my Social Media and getting my brandname out there; this did wonders and opened up all kinds of new opportunities!
Oscar, bonsaiempire.com

Using your Social Media

Social Media are incredibly large networks and you have direct access to them. Use them as a platforms for your thoughts and ideas, start discussions and communicate with your followers. The more active you are and the more interesting the things you say and share, the more loyal your following will become. This is brand building and networking at the same time.

Using your Newsletter

Sending out newsletters to your subscribers can be great way to gain authority in your field. But it has to be interesting. Sharing only updates from your website will not do it, but if you send out a monthly newsletter with lots of cool and interesting information, links and ideas, that might just work.

Alright, what's next?

You know how to gain authority and understand why you need it. Well done, now let's look at how you can grow your network.

Build your network to ensure growth

If you're serious about your startup, building your network is what you need to think of. You covered the basics of making money online by building your website and filling it with great content, time to take things to the next level. Without a network, you won't be able to keep growing. You network will proof to be crucial in building an extended link network, but much more important, in setting up partnerships and in becoming an authority in your field.

Build your network

Alright, so how do I build my network? That depends much on what niche you're in, but it always comes to one thing; meeting and being acquainted with the right people. You can get in touch with them through Social Media, but meeting them in person during events/lectures/etc will be much more effective in building relationships.

Attending events
Most likely there will be many events you can think of that are relevant to your startup. Try to find out which events are held near you and attend them. Cover them on your blog, conduct interviews, make a film, talk about it on your social media, etc. Or hire a stand

and present yourself. Know which people are important for your network and try to meet them.

Build your online network
Post comments on influential articles written on your field. Engage in discussions. Email the author with an intelligent question. Start conversations!

Join or start a workshop or masterclass
Join lectures, workshops or masterclasses or even start one yourself. Engage in discussions or introduce topics to discuss in which you know you can make a contribution.

Build and solidify your Social Network

I can't say this enough, Social Networks are key success factors to your startup and you need to take them very serious. Engage with your followers/fans, start discussions, ask them for their opinion and connect with people important to you. Building your Social network can benefit the expansion of your 'offline' network.

My website was quite famous and had a lot of traffic, but it really took off when my network started to become well established. Partnerships I benefit from as well as media coverage are all the result of my personal network.
Oscar, bonsaiempire.com

Network; check!

You understand the importance of your network,
let's start looking at ways to start earning more!

Step 6: Earn more

Welcome to the final step: adding additional methods to Monetize your Website

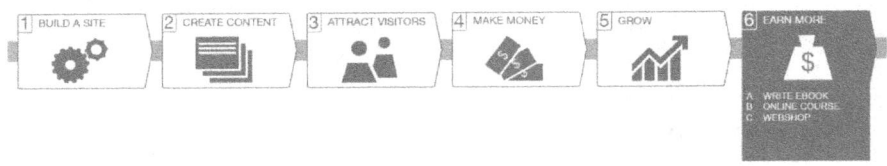

Last step already. This is where we start looking at additional ways to make money with your website. Think about writing an eBook, creating an online course or starting a webshop.

How to write an eBook and make money

Writing an eBook can be a great way to monetize your website. Yes, it'll be a lot of work to create and publish your book, but the rewards can be substantial. Your eBook sales will boost your monetization efforts but also help you to increase your authority.

So how do you write an eBook? How do you publish it? And how do you make it successful? Let's get started.

Writing your eBook

I'm assuming you have a topic in mind. Something you're passionate about as well as knowledgeable. But where do we start?

Before you start writing you need to think about what your target audience is and what you want them to learn from reading your eBook. Is there a unifying theme of your book, and how can it be structured into chapters? You will also need to decide on what style you wish to use (personal, motivational or professional). These considerations are mostly dictated by your topic and audience, so no rocket science here, but making these decisions before you start will save you a lot of time later on in the process.

Start with structure

No matter what the topic of your eBook is, or what the point you want to bring across is, your book needs structure. Before you start thinking in terms of chapters, hold on for just a little bit because we need to think about it first. Let's start with creating a mindmap:

1. Write down the topic of your book in the center of a piece of paper.
2. Now add all the ideas, sub-topics and other points that come to mind around your central topic.
3. Ask a few friends or colleagues to add to this list (explain your topic and ask them to share what comes to mind when thinking about it).
4. Now structure the points on your list, by creating clusters.

With this mindmap you have an idea of how to structure your topic into subtopics. But most likely, your mindmap is big, so you will need to decide on the scope of your book before we can proceed. So what should be in your book, and what not? You have already decided on the audience of your eBook, and most likely, you know your audience because you engage with them in your network and on Social Media. So ask yourself, what is it they want? Keeping this in mind, return to your mindmap, and start eliminating points that are outside the scope of your eBook.

The last step of creating the structure of your eBook is to put the points that remain on your mindmap in a logical sequence. What is the starting point of your book (what do your readers need to know about first) and how do you proceed from there all the way towards the end?

Once your mindmap is structured we only need to add an introduction and conclusion, perhaps an appendix, and you got yourself a table of contents for your eBook!

Software you will need to write your eBook

Unless you are a skilled InDesign designer (which only very few people are) and unless you focus exclusively on iBooks (in that case use iBooks Author), I urge you to keep things simple. Use your normal Word or Pages software to write your texts.

There is one thing you need to keep in mind: once you finish writing, your texts will need to be converted into several eBook formats. In these formats, your text structuring options are very limited. This means you need to keep your texts simple:

Do not use:
Tables
Indents
Aligned images
Page background colors
Columns
Headers or footers

You can use:
Headings
Bullet points
Numbered lists
Bold, Italic and Underlined texts

Start writing

You have created your mind map and used it to arrive at the table of contents of your book. So you know what you will need to write about, you simply need to get started.

Everyone has a different method, but what works for me is to skip the introduction and start writing the chapters first, from start to end. For each individual chapter I start with making an outline, to make sure I write with structure. Did I mention structure is important (yes I did!). This outline consists of the chapter's title and its subtitles, and preferably sub-subtitles. This article you are reading right now? I added all the titles before I created the texts, and I hope you noticed it got structure!

Whatever works for you. But get started!

Adding graphics

No matter what your topic is, your book needs graphical elements. Think about adding illustrations, photos, infographics and diagrams. These elements help structure your content and bring your point across in a clear way. People like graphics much more than they like text.

Probably, you are no expert at creating graphics, so you will need to find someone who can help you. There are a few websites that offer free graphics (try GraphicStock) but you can also hire someone to create custom work using Fiverr.

Things to keep in mind when you're done writing

Finished writing? Well done! There are a few things to look at next:

Your eBook's title
Your title is a very important factor for people deciding whether or not to purchase your book. It needs to cover your book's content, but more importantly, it needs to draw attention of your audience. So what is it they want?
Why don't you surf to Amazon's site and open the Kindle store, browse to the category where you will most likely publish your book as well, and have a look around. What titles are published that you find interesting?

Most likely, some book covers attract your attention before you even look at titles (we will talk about your cover next), but what you will notice is that the cover thumbnails are small. This means that your title needs to be short so that you can use a large font.

Conclusion: you need a title that attracts the attention of your audience and it needs to be short.

Example of eBook covers.

Your eBook's cover
Welcome to the single most important step of your eBook's success. Competition on stores like Amazon and iBooks is huge, so your eBook cover needs to stand out. Go back to Amazon's Kindle store and look at the covers; which ones do you like, and why?

Most likely you won't design your own eBook cover, a website I highly recommend to have yours designed is Fiverr (and it will cost only $5). But before you ask someone to design it you will need to have decided on colors, show some designs you like and have a title ready. The title should cover a quarter or even half your cover, in order to make sure that it is readable also on stores like Amazon where it will be displayed as a small thumbnail.

The cover needs to be at least 625 x 1000 pixels, or taller.

Formats: ePub, Mobi and PDF

Before you can start to publish your eBook you will need to convert your Word/Pages file into several formats.

ePub
This is the open standard for the industry and accepted by most publishers, including Nook and iBooks. If you created your eBook using Word you will need to convert it. There are several ways to do so, but I recommend using an opensource program named Calibre. Using this program you can easily convert your file. Apple's program Pages can export files into the ePub format directly, if for some reason this doesn't work out you can also use Calibre for Mac. Always check the resulting ePub file carefully, as some design features of your book might have been changed during the conversion. Remember that ePub only offers very simple design options, as we mentioned above in the paragraph on software.

Mobi
This is Amazon's format and unfortunately they don't accept ePub. They do offer a tool to convert ePub into Mobi format, called KindleGen. Be sure to check the resulting Mobi file for design errors before you publish it. Recently Amazon enabled the upload of ePub files, to process them automatically into their Mobi format. Do check the result before you publish.

PDF
Both Word and Pages can easily export your texts into the PDF format, which will be useful if you decide to sell your eBook directly to your website visitors.

Setting the price of your eBook

The price of your eBook should depend on its length, quality and competition. Unfortunately, I don't have the winning formula for you, so you will have to experiment to establish what works for you. Have a look at the Kindle store to have an idea of what prices are common for similar books. Setting your price above the competition might signal quality, but this will have to match with your future reviews. Setting a lower price might be a smart strategy to launch your eBook and to receive your first, much needed, reviews.

Amazon and Nook offer the best royalty rates when you price your eBook between $2,99 and $9,99 so you probably want to respect that.

I wrote an eBook on starting with growing Bonsai and there were a lot of Bonsai eBooks on Amazon already. Their covers were colorful and had a lot of text on them, so I decided to go for a solid black cover with a big title and an absolutely stunning image. This turned out to be very successful and my eBook's cover attracts most attention. My audience is people not yet growing Bonsai trees, so the title of my book is "Bonsai, a beginners guide".
Oscar, bonsaiempire.com

Publishing your eBook

Finally we reach the best part; publishing and selling your eBook. You can publish your eBook directly at the largest stores (the big three) but also through intermediates that will publish your book for you to many stores. The latter comes with an additional price tag, but it can be convenient. Finally, you can also sell your eBook directly to your website's visitors as PDF.

I recommend self publishing to the big three to maximize your royalty share, and using an intermediate in case you also want your eBook published to the many other stores out there. If your website has traffic, definitely offer your book as PDF file to sell it directly to your visitors as well.

The big three

The big three are Amazon (Kindle), Barnes and Noble (Nook) and Apple iTunes (iBooks). Amazon is the largest in the USA with a market share of around 60%, Nook and iBooks follow and are about the same size (around 15%). This means that the big three combined have a market share of close to 90% in the USA.

All three stores have self publishing platforms and offer royalties around 65%, which is much better than the royalties you would receive from selling printed books. Another convenience is that with self publishing at the big three, you don't need to purchase an ISBN for your eBook.

amazonkindle

eBook Publishing at Amazon's Kindle

Self publishing your eBook at Amazon is easy and won't take much of your time. If your eBook's price is between $2,99 and $9,99 your royalty share is 70%, which is pretty good. You will also need to pay for delivery costs of your eBook, so in the end you will make slightly less than the 70% share.

You do need to consider a few options they offer when publishing your book, so keep reading:

1. Sign up at Amazon's self publishing platform called KDP.
2. You will need to agree with their terms and then provide your details, including bank account and possibly taxpayer ID.
3. Once your account is set up, click on "Add new title"
4. You need to decide whether or not to enroll in the KDP Select. The advantage is that you make additional money from the Kindle Unlimited program and have access to promotional tools, also, you will most likely get those much wanted first book reviews faster. The downside is that for 90 days you can't publish your book elsewhere. If you book is targeting the USA it often makes sense to enroll.
5. Add your book's details like title, subtitle and description.
6. At "Publishing Rights" you most likely need to select that your book is not a public work (if you hold the rights to everything inside your book).
7. Pick two categories for your book, the first is the most important.
8. Add your cover.
9. Add your book file (your .mobi file).
10. In the next step set your price.
11. Kindle match book: only applicable if you have a hard-copy version as well.
12. Kindle lending: this enables sharing your eBook between befriended customers. I usually enable this feature, especially when I first publish an eBook.

13. Click on Publish and you're done! Amazon will check your book and within a day your book is available in the Kindle store.
14. On the KDP homepage you can copy the direct link to your eBook per Amazon country, use these links when promoting your book.

eBook Publishing at iTunes and its iBooks

Self publishing your eBook at iBooks is also relatively straight forward. You earn a 70% royalty on your sales and iTunes doesn't charge delivery cost, so your earnings per sold book will be higher than with Amazon.

1. Get your AppleID.
2. Enable your AppleID for iTunes Connect.
3. You will need to provide your personal details, including bank account and possibly taxpayer ID.
4. Download the software iTunes Producer, this is the program used to add your eBook to the iBooks store.
5. Open iTunes Producer and create a new Book.
6. Add your eBook details, including title, subtitle, description, publisher and publication date.
7. Upload your cover photo and up to five screenshots of attractive pages from your eBook.
8. In the next step, set up the price of your eBook for all or for individual regions.
9. In the last step, select your eBook file (the .epub file).
10. Once approved you can upload your book to iTunes / iBooks. It will take some time before it starts to appear in the iTunes stores worldwide.
11. To link to your eBook in the iTunes stores you can use iTunes Link Maker.

eBook Publishing at Nook

Publishing your eBook at Nook is easy. Your royalty share is 65% for products priced between $2,99 - $9,99.

1. Create your account at Nook Press.
2. You will need to provide your personal details, including bank account and possibly taxpayer ID in your account.
3. Click on "Create a project" and insert your eBook title.
4. Upload your eBook (your .epub file)
5. Nook will search your ePub file for the title and other data, but make sure to check this carefully.
6. Upload your cover image.
7. Insert all the required data and select the categories (up to 5).
8. Set your eBook price and choose whether or not to enable DRM (protection of your file; I suggest you don't use this feature as it will annoy your customers).
9. Publish your eBook and wait for a few hours for your book to be accepted.
10. To get the direct link to your Nook sales page, open your eBook project page and click on "View Nook Book product page".

Other eBook publishers and intermediates

If self publishing is too much effort for you, using the services of an intermediate can be convenient. You only need to signup once and upload your eBook file, and they will publish and distribute to all the eBook stores. They can even help you with designing a cover, though I recommend to save money by arranging this yourself. In case you have chosen to self publish your eBook at the big three there are several more stores where you can also publish your book using an intermediate.

There are two famous intermediates, BookBaby and SmashWords. BookBaby offers better royalty rates but they charge a signup fee starting at $99. SmashWords is a free service, but they take part of your royalties. Compare both services and their prices on their websites. Simplicissimus is another service in which you can freely select the stores where you want your eBook published, convenient if you wish to combine self publishing and their services.

A few other markets for eBooks

The USA leads the way in terms of eBook sales, but the eBook markets in several other countries are growing:

Spanish: iBooks (40%), Amazon (30%) and Casa del Libro (15%).

German: Amazon (50%), Thalia+Weltbild (34%) and iBooks (10%).

Italian: Amazon leads, with iBooks, Kobo and IBS following.

Dutch: Bol.com (80%) and iBooks (10%).

I have my eBook available in several languages. The English version is by far the most important, but the Spanish and German books do pretty well too. If you have translations of your content, make sure to publish your eBook in multiple languages.
Oscar, starttomonetize.com

Maximizing your eBook sales

You've published your eBook, so what's next?

Creating your sales page
Although your eBook is available on the stores of Amazon and iBooks, it makes sense to drive as much traffic to those pages as you possibly can from your website. It makes even more sense to offer your visitors a chance to buy your eBook directly from you as well; so sell your book in PDF format on a sales page!

Your sales page should include pictures of your book, a description and some reviews, as well as links to the stores where your eBook can be purchased. If you wish to sell a PDF file from your website you can arrange this yourself by installing a digital file sales extension (available for both Joomla! and WordPress) or use an external service like Selz or Sellfy.

The importance of reviews
Customer reviews on stores including Amazon, iBooks and Nook are very important to drive sales. At some stores it is possible to add a review without buying the book, but be sure to expect a banned account if all your reviews are non-paid. Most publishers even buy positive reviews, but this is a risky practice.

What I do after launching an eBook is offering fans on Social Media a free copy if they write a review. Setting a low introduction price of your eBook might also be a good way to get those first reviews.

eBook done, what's next?

Now that your eBook is published, think about other way to make some additional money with your site, like creating an online course.

How to create an Online Course and make money

Creating an online course is a lot of work. You need to create the course material (that usually means several lectures/movies as well as learning materials), set up your eLearning platform and do your marketing. Having said that, it truly is a great way to make money online and it will help you gain authority in your field as well.

So how do you make and sell your online course? Let's get started.

Creating an online course, how does that work?

eLearning has been around since the internet started and by now, most topics you can think of have an online course designed specifically for them. Several universities offer complete studies online, but the most popular courses on the internet cover topics including learning how to trade stocks, how to play poker or how to use software like Photoshop. Several platforms have been launched to accommodate these courses, the most popular is Udemy.

But what exactly is an online course then? In an online course students go through the course curriculum just like they would go through a textbook; step by step. The curriculum consists of several chapters that can be taught using lectures (with a teacher on screen, or screen-recorded film with a voiceover) or by using learning materials like an eBook or PDF files. Each chapter can be concluded with an online quiz and a certificate can be granted when the entire course is successfully completed. Try a free course on Udemy to understand how it works.

How to create the course

The first step of creating your course is to decide on its topic, scope and curriculum. I assume you have the topic already so let's start with looking at scope.

Say your course will be targeted at beginners at some topic, in this case it will make sense to include a rather large scope of subjects, but to limit the complexity or depth of the content. This way you cover the basics and students will gain an understanding of what the main topic is about. In case your course is an advanced class the scope will be much more limited, while the topics you do cover will be more complex and detailed. This way, students increase their knowledge on a specific topic.

The curriculum depends largely on your topic and the scope you decide on. Make sure to structure your course very well; create a logical flow from the introduction towards the concluding chapter. The curriculum will be one of the most important things that visitors look at when deciding to pay for your course.

When you have decided on the topic, scope and curriculum it is time to start creating the learning materials and/or lectures.

Creating the learning materials

Most online courses consist largely of filmed lectures, but offering additional learning materials will help structure the course and function as useful reference material. Learning materials include, but are not limited to, textbooks, eBooks, PDF files, cheatsheets and tools needed for the course.

Another benefit of offering additional materials is that you can sell your course as an all-in package. This is very useful for marketing your course.

Creating the lectures

Lectures are the backbone of online courses and creating them is difficult and time consuming. A lecture can be a teacher in front of a camera explaining the subjects, or it can be a screen-recorded film using a voiceover. The latter is often used to explain how software works (it takes you through the steps performed on screen) and is much easier to create than filming lectures. To film a teacher in front of the camera means you need equipment (a HD camera, quality sound recording and lighting) as well as a location and a person who has teaching and acting skills. Your course topic largely determines what options you have.

What follows is a introduction in filming, I will provide links to quality resources for additional in-depth information.

Scripting
Educating is difficult enough, so you will need good scripts to create structure in your lessons. Scripting means that you write down what you will talk about in each lesson, which can be done using keywords but usually you will need to write down your exact texts.

As soon as you start filming you will realize how difficult acting is and how much you need your script, especially when recording-time is limited. Investing time in writing your scripts will save a lot of time when you start filming.

A good script brings structure and good flow in your texts. Think about it; a spoken text has no headings, bullet points and numbered lists, so it is quite difficult to make your point. This can be partly resolved by editing textual elements into the movie, but you need to think about these things when creating your script.

So how do you write a good film script?

Take the first lecture you will film and write down the main point of this lesson. Also write down a few key take-aways, things that your students should be able to remember from your lesson. With your main point and key take-aways you have just created your film's structure! Around this main structure you can now start writing your lines of text. A good film needs scripting, but it shouldn't feel scripted, so use plain speak and keep things natural.

Don't be afraid to add personality to it, remember your favorite teacher from high school? Exactly, he wasn't boring! You are the expert in your field and your students don't want a robot in front of the camera, speaking robot language.

Finally, read your scripts out loud. Only then will you understand why I just said you need plain and natural speak. Written lines of text sound very different from spoken text. More information can be found at the great resources over at Wistia.

Filming
Got your scripts all worked out? Than let's start filming.

In case you can use screen-recorded lessons all you need is a computer, a microphone and a simple piece of free software (CamStudio). With this software you can film what happens on your computer screen; like how Photoshop works, or a slideshow about any topic. While it records your screen live, it also records your voice, and with the script you just created you have everything you need to start creating the film. All it takes is a little practice.

When screen-recording doesn't make sense for your topic, prepare for a much steeper learning curve and bigger investment in both time and effort. The scope of this article is too limited to discuss how to film in detail, but I will explain some of the basics and link to other resources for additional reading.

Let's start with location and light; if your movie will be shot inside that will simplify things a bit as you won't have to focus on ambient noise and variations in light intensity. Your lesson can be recorded as an actual lecture, in front of a whiteboard, or it can be done in a studio-setting. Either way, you will need to make sure there is enough light, preferably diffuse and from different sides.

Next up is your filming equipment. Shooting HD has become standard and even your iPhone can do it (and do it well if zooming is not required and you have the FilmMic app). Otherwise any digital camera will do the job. You will need a solid tripod to put your camera on, which is tall enough to place your camera at eye-level.

Deciding on how to record sound is much more difficult. If you will be recording while standing close to your camera, your camera's mic might do. But probably not, and definitely not when you move away from the camera even by a little bit. It will sound hollow and it will catch a lot of ambient sound, especially when you are outside. Using a Lav Mic (clip-on) is convenient and inexpensive but much more conveniently, you can use your iPhone. You will need to hang it in front of you though, just above you. And if you film with an iPhone, that means you need two.

Much more on all this can be learned at Wistia's learning center (free).

Editing
The final step of production is editing. If you have a Mac, you have a very good editing software installed called iMovie. It is easy to work with but powerful enough to create excellent movies. Windows has a free software available too, called MovieMaker. The thing is, with

both options you will have to go through the learning curve and invest some time in it. You always have the option to outsource the editing and if your filmed lessons are not very complex this shouldn't be very expensive.

One other thing you need to think about is music. Your movies need background music. Good background music fits with your lesson's content and is calm enough never to grab the attention away from your voice. Search the FMA website for much more copyright-free music.

For my website I created an online course to introduce the basics of Bonsai. Coming up with a good curriculum and structure saved us tons of time when we started scripting and filming. Lots of fun, but lots of work.
Oscar, bonsaiempire.com

How to sell the course

You have four options to sell your course. It might make sense to combine options, but that will depend on what you wish to achieve; are you focusing on maximizing sales or profits? Let's investigate the options first.

1) External platforms

There are several websites that offer both the learning platform and prospective students. By far the biggest one is Udemy, with over 4 million registered students. You can create your course for free and upload all the movies and learning materials you created.

If you send students from your website and social media to your course on Udemy, you receive about 97% of the price of your course. If students enroll in your course from within the Udemy platform you receive about 50%. These rates deteriorate in case you enable affiliate sales or ad program sales. It is the biggest platform available, so if you like to benefit from their large student base, you will need to accept the 50% share. The only real alternative to Udemy is SkillShare.

2) Whitelabel platforms

Whitelabel platforms offer the same kind of platform that Udemy offers, but are entirely branded and operated by yourself. Usually you pay the whitelabel platform a fixed fee per month and a transaction fee to cover the payment costs. If you have a lot of visitors and a large network of Social Media, offering your course through a whitelabel will make sense as you keep most of your profits in your own pockets.

There are several platforms available, all with different pricing options, so compare a few. I like Patience, Fedora, Thinkific, Kunerango and Pathwright.

3) Whitelabel extensions for Joomla! or WordPress

If you don't want to pay monthly fees and don't mind setting up payment channels yourself, buying an eLearning extension for Joomla! or WordPress is an option. The available extensions don't look and feel as well designed as the whitelabel options above though. Guru is the extension you need for Joomla, CoursePress or Courseware are your options for WordPress.

4) Sell as digital download or DVD

Finally you have the option not to use a platform, but to sell your entire course as a digital file or on a DVD.

Selling your course as a digital file has the benefit that you can sell it easily through PayPal (using a simple plugin to your website) or through a service like Selz or Sellfy. The downside is that you don't offer your students a learning platform, they will only be able to watch your movies and read your learning materials, instead of going through individual classes with quizzes.

Selling your course on a DVD, perhaps with a very simple interface added to it, might be a good way for you to resell your course to (online) stores. Depending on how many you produce, the cost of pressing the DVD's will be $5 to $15 per piece. This could be a great strategy to make your course widely available. Wholesaling your DVD means you will need to adjust your price, as shops normally add 100% to your wholesale price.

It might make sense to offer your course first through a whitelabel option, and wait with offering it on platforms like Udemy for some time to maximize your returns.
Oscar, starttomonetize.com

How to market the course

Thought creating a course was a lot of work? Try selling it! The obvious starting point is to use your following of both your website and your Social Media networks. Explain them why your course is a great way to learn, how useful it will be to them and how well it's put together. Most platforms offer discount coupons, which you could use to drive traffic into your course when you have just published it. Similar to eBooks, your first reviews will be crucial for the success of your course.

Once your fans know about your course you will need to become more creative in doing your marketing. Perhaps there are ways to receive attention from the press, or from blogs that write about topics similar to your course. You can consider writing an official press release to be send out to all these blogs, or by using the services of PRPress.

Online course created.

Well done, this was a lot of work but I am sure it will be worth it. How about you consider starting an online shop? Next step...

Starting an Online Store and making money

Starting an online shop is a lot of work and it requires an ongoing effort, but I consider it the ultimate way to monetize your website and the potential can be significant. Since it's so much work you need to think about what exactly you would have to set up and what your ongoing efforts will be, and decide if it'll be worth your time. I don't want to put you off, but I do want you to be realistic. Let's get to it.

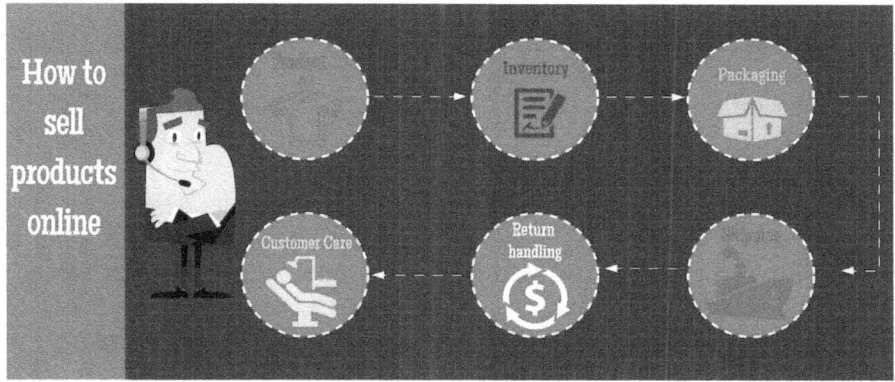

Things to consider before you start selling online

Before you start investing both money and time in setting up a webshop you need to think about what you want to sell and how to do that.

Deciding what to sell
Most likely you have a good idea of what you want to sell, but you need to realize that your product's features will designate how complex your shop will be to set up. Selling digital files for example is much more convenient than selling large bulky items. Selling high value products with a healthy profit margin is often much more attractive than selling large quantities of low-margin products. The

product you decide to sell designates the effort you have to put into it and how much profit you will make. Think this through!

Deciding how to sell
Let's have a look at the options available for selling your products, sorted by the amount of investment needed to get started (low to high):

1. Digital products
Selling a digital product is the option with the least amount of effort required to get started, as you only need to set up a payment system and send out automated download links to customers. You can use a service like Selz, or install an extension to your Joomla! or WordPress site to handle the payments and downloads.

2. Drop-Ship agreement
Several companies offer Drop-Ship agreements. Basically you are reselling whitelabel products of another company, under your own name and from your webshop. Every order that is paid in your shop will be packaged and shipped by your partner. Your partner will also be responsible for product descriptions and images, saving you a lot of time. I don't know a platform where Drop-Ship partners present themselves, so you will have to Google for it, or approach companies in your network to propose a partnership.

3. Sell it yourself with fulfillment outsourced
If you don't have a Drop-Ship option available, or when you need more flexibility and ownership, you can run your online shop yourself and outsource the fulfillment process. You pay a company to keep your inventory and ship the products to your customers. They can even handle returns and customer complaints/questions for you. There are several large fulfillment companies, a familiar one is Amazon and another option is Shipwire. Shop around to get a feeling for the fees involved in outsourcing. Depending on how much you sell and depending on your product dimensions, it will cost at least $5 dollar per order, excluding shipment fees.

4. Sell and ship yourself
The most resource intensive option is to do it all yourself. You create your webshop and handle the inventory, shipments, returns and customer service.

Testing before investing

It makes a lot of sense to start small, testing the waters before you start investing. By now you have selected the product or products you like to sell, and if you have easy access to them in small quantities, try selling these first. Even if that means you don't make a profit on these sales. You can use Google Adwords to generate traffic to your sales page to test if people are interested in your product and how much money you need to invest in marketing in order to generate sales. And you will have important insights in questions like: How do people respond to your product? How many returns did you get? What price worked best?

Ultimately, you need to decide if your efforts will lead to earning a healthy profit. With the "testing before investing" approach you know what to expect.

On my website I offer paid downloads of my eBook. Sales are good and the process is automated. At one of my other websites I run a webshop with a large assortment of products, but I outsource the fulfillment. I try to make sure that I don't link myself to the processing of orders, to stay focused on setting up new projects.
Oscar, bonsaiempire.com

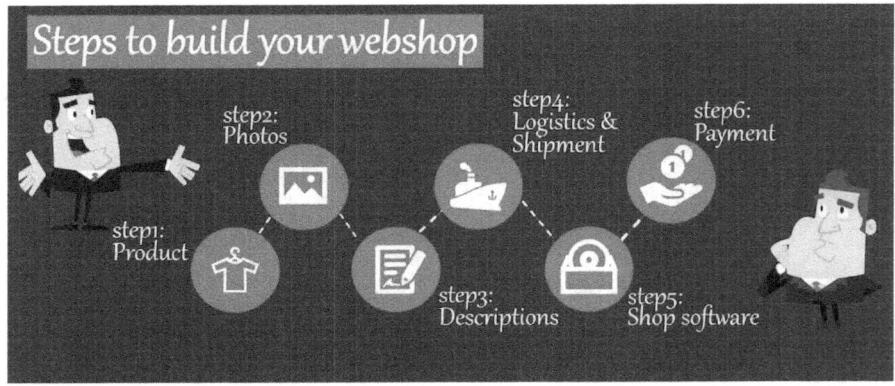

Starting your webshop

When you are setting up your online store several steps need to be taken, think about making product photos, arranging your logistics, finding a shop platform and accepting payments. It will depend on what option you chose above in the "Deciding how to sell" section which of the following steps apply to you.

Products
Most likely you know where to get your products already, but in order to make enough profits, your cost price as well as product quality needs to be solid. Shop around before deciding to place a large order, and as I said before, try testing the waters first with a small batch.

Your options for getting your products include importing, purchasing at a wholesaler, partnering with someone who creates the products or creating them yourself.

Product photos and descriptions
No matter what product you sell, you need quality photos and descriptions. Especially products that people don't know very well need several photos to take away concerns of your customers.

Show your product from different angles and include a few closeups, you might even want to add a 360-degree photo or a short movie. Product photography is difficult though and most people I know outsourced this step.

Writing descriptions and titles for your products is another key factor in boosting sales. Not only is this important for your customers, the textual descriptions are key ranking factors for Google. Most often it makes sense to write a short description of 2-3 lines, and add a detailed version of at least 10 lines. Make sure to add other information separately, including your product's dimensions and features.

Logistics and shipment

We looked at logistics and shipments when we discussed the options to sell your products. You will have to decide whether or not you will sell your own products or resell someone else's, and in case you sell you own products you need to decide whether or not to outsource the fulfillment (warehousing and shipment).

Accepting payments

Offering payments is relatively straightforward, although this depends on what markets you sell your products in. Offering PayPal payments will suffice in a few countries, but in most cases you will need to be able to accept credit cards as well. For this, you will need to register with a Payment Service Provider (PSP) like Authorize.net. They will charge you a fee per payment, usually in line with the actual costs for the transfer with Visa or MasterCard.

Enabling these payments in your online shop is easy, usually the required plugins are pre-installed, so that you only need to add your account data.

Finally, think about how much work this is

By now you should have a pretty good understanding of the amount of work it takes to set up and run an online shop. Think about it once again; does the profit potential of your shop justify the amount of effort required to set it up? If your answer it yes, go for it!

I always set up online stores with automation in mind; I like setting up new projects but don't want to be that guy who packs and ships the products. Outsourcing can be expensive, but it enables me to focus on project development.
Oscar, starttomonetize.com

Choosing your shop system

You have several options available to set up your online shop. If you have a Joomla! or WordPress site you can choose from several extensions, most of which are free and easy to set up. There are also companies that offer all-in eCommerce solutions, so that you don't need any skills at creating websites.

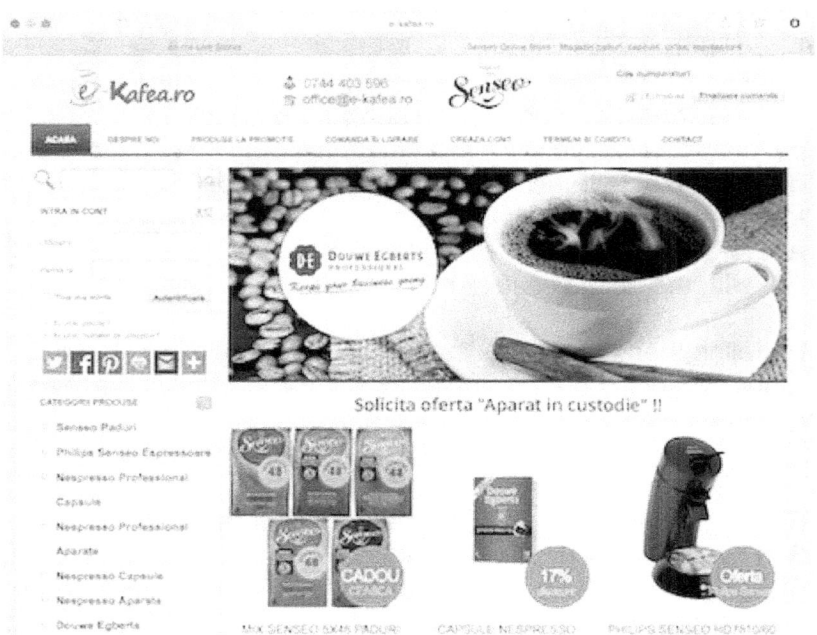

Virtuemart shop

Jigo Shop

Wix shop

Magento shop

All-Inclusive eCommerce Services

The most used eCommerce service is Shopify, and their offer is great. You can choose between different designs and easily enable payment options and shipment fees. You pay a monthly fee and transaction costs per order. All in all, a great option if you have no skills at all to set up a store using Joomla! or WordPress.

Alternatives to Shopify include Wix, BigCommerce, Goodsie, Jumpseller and Volusion.

Extensions to Joomla! and WordPress

If you chose to use Joomla! or WordPress in one of the previous steps (Creating your website) it will make sense to use one of their extensions to create your online shop. You already know how these Content Management Systems work so it won't take you much time to set up their shoppingcart extensions. Mostly, these extensions are free so that it will save you the monthly fees that eCommerce services charge.

For Joomla! I recommend the Virtuemart extension, which is an all-in eCommerce solution with all the plugins needed to set up your payment and shipment options. An alternative would be HikaShop. For WordPress I recommend TheCartPress, Jigoshop or WooCommerce.

Shop software systems

If you prefer not to create your shop as an extension to either Joomla! or WordPress (most likely because you need a more powerful platform) Magento is the system you need. Magento is an incredibly versatile and powerful shop software, the choice of most large online stores, including Nike and Gant. The downside is that its many options make the system complex to set up and you need a powerful server to be able to run it. An alternative to Magento, though less complete, is OpenCart.

If your shop will be large and you need endless features and options, you can't get around Magento. If your needs are somewhat more 'normal' you are just as well off with Joomla! or WordPress extensions.

Online shop; check!

You set up your shop and started selling, well done! Congratulations! That was the last step.

Conclusion

I never said it was easy, right? Going through the steps towards making money online is hard work. But your investments will pay off on the long run and once your website is built, promoted and monetized you start seeing the results.

I certainly hope this guide was what you were looking for and even more important, I hope you got started with your own website by now. Too many people I met always got stuck at the very first step and never started anything. But not you.

Questions? Drop me a line at info (at) starttomonetize.com.

Liked this book? Please help me by adding your review!

www.ingramcontent.com/pod-product-compliance
Lightning Source LLC
Chambersburg PA
CBHW070809180526
45168CB00002B/545